Quiet Cop

Social Tactics for Law Enforcement Professionals

Stephen J. Sampson, Ph.D.

Published by: HRD Press, Inc.
22 Amherst Road
Amherst, MA 01002
800-822-2801 (U.S. and Canada)
413-253-3488
413-253-3490 (fax)
www.hrdpress.com

ISBN 978-1-61014-411-7

Production services by Jean Miller
Cover design by Michael J. Davis
Editorial work by James Cabe

TABLE OF CONTENTS

PREFACE

Over many decades, the term "peace officer" has been replaced by terms such as "police officer" and "law enforcement officer." A growing number of people in society equate the terms "police" and "enforcement" as being non-trustworthy, unethical, and/or militaristic. Law enforcement officers in modern society must work together at every level to build trust and legitimacy within the communities they are sworn to serve and protect. Building positive relationships with communities is imperative to improving the perception of law enforcement in the United States of America.

Are you an officer who would like to improve the image and perception of the law enforcement profession? Are you frustrated or concerned by stereotypes that all officers are unethical, racist, and/or not trustworthy?

The traditional law enforcement training paradigm places primary focus on knowledge of laws and tactical training. Very limited instruction in such training paradigms focus on effective officer-to-citizen communication. While *physical* tactical training is essential in the law enforcement profession, the purpose of this book is to introduce effective ways for law enforcement officers to communicate, using knowledge, which emphasizes techniques geared towards building trust and building a rapport with someone. Essentially, the skills and methods contained within this book will teach the law enforcement officer peace-keeping skills that will ultimately build rapport and better, long-lasting, and positive relationships with citizens. This book places a focus on advanced social tactics (how to talk to people) involving officer encounters with the public. These tactics focus on almost every possible social encounter an officer or deputy

1

may have during the course of their daily duties. Mainly, this includes contact with citizens, witnesses, victims, suspects, offenders, and persons who are in crisis or suffering from mental illness.

Officers are all alike in that each can think back to "that first time" they were tested in the performance of their duties, either by a physical or verbal threat. Most law enforcement officers can think back to a time when the words they chose to speak during a particular incident drastically escalated the situation, causing problems that could have been avoided. If the words they spoke and their demeanor at the time had been different, there would have been a better outcome. Most veteran officers learn very early in their careers how to effectively communicate with other people, which drastically reduces the need for non-lethal or lethal force. Of course, there are times when the actions of others are so violent that officers have no choice but to stop a threat rather than attempt to de-escalate.

Knowledge and understanding one's lawful authority is imperative for an officer to communicate effectively and with confidence. Possessing the knowledge of how to handle most situations allows officers to speak more confidently (with knowledge) and ultimately achieve better results.

Why This Book?

The majority of complaints against officers that are received and investigated by law enforcement agencies are due to how the officer reportedly treated an individual or group of individuals during an incident. In many (but not all) cases, the officer(s) could have prevented a complaint from being filed if they had communicated in a more effective manner with the individual(s) on scene.

The content of this book addresses many of the different encounters that law enforcement officers have during the course of their duties each day. Examples of common encounters are provided and ways of effectively communicating while also being safe and maintaining physical tactics for safety are discussed.

It is the intent of this book to reduce the number of complaints received by a law enforcement agency and for individual officers to build more positive and trustworthy relationships with citizens in the community.

Overview

When the book *Quiet Cop: Social Tactics for Law Enforcement Professionals* is presented to attendees in a classroom setting, the instructor will utilize four methods of instruction:

1. Tell
2. Show
3. Role Play
4. Input

The learning plan is both simple and systematic. First, the instructor will **TELL** class attendees what the learning module is all about. Second, they will **SHOW** the skill that will be learned in the module by demonstrating its use through instructor demonstration and sometimes a video simulation. Third, the instructor will have class attendees learn the skill by practicing it in a **ROLE PLAY** activity. Fourth, class attendees will have **INPUT** into the learning both by evaluating the role player and then having an opportunity to discuss the activity thoroughly and give their thoughts and ideas based on observations of the role play scenario.

Like any training, failure can be programmed as well as success. The key to success is the willingness of each class attendee to participate without distraction.

Chapter 1

Introduction

Basic Knowledge

Law enforcement officers must possess knowledge to effectively serve and protect the community. Recruits in mandate certification training receive instruction on a predetermined curriculum that is intended to provide basic knowledge to perform the duties of a law enforcement officer. Most officers will attest that the information learned in basic mandate training begins their foundation of knowledge, but the bulk of their basic knowledge came from hands-on training within a program equal or similar to a Field Training Officer (FTO) program.

Possessing basic knowledge is imperative and serves as an introduction to not only knowing one's job, but also building confidence to effectively perform the duties of that job. The curriculum for basic mandate certification programs are predetermined by each state's applicable governing authority, typically a Peace Officer Standards and Training (POST) council. Additionally, the number of hours to obtain certification varies, although each state has a mandatory minimum number of hours in attendance required, along with other requirements, to successfully earn certification as a certified officer. This essentially is where it all begins for the officer with regard to building the foundation of knowledge to be effective in one's career.

After completing basic mandate certification training and during training in the field, officers continue to grow and build upon the basic knowledge they learned in a mandate certification curriculum. At this point, knowledge transitions from learning the basics about the job to learning the basics about how the employing agency wants their officers to perform the job. Agency-specific policies and procedures are introduced to employees during training in the field and this new knowledge is added to the foundation of information learned while attending basic mandate training. Over time, the employees begin to build knowledge and enhanced confidence to perform their assigned duties.

It is essential for law enforcement officers to continuously strive to enhance their knowledge as it provides the foundation for improved confidence and effective communication with others. When officers begin employment with an agency, it is imperative that they thoroughly understand federal, state, and local laws and also the employing agency's policies and procedures. Learning and comprehending laws, regulations, policies, and procedures are crucial first steps in building a foundation of knowledge for newly-sworn officers to effectively perform their duties.

The direction of law enforcement has changed over recent decades. Law enforcement officers were initially called peace officers. This shift was due to officers possibly having too much discretion in their application of the law when they were called peace officers. By switching to the term law enforcement officers, the primary focus became enforcing the law and not necessarily the peace.

Today, officers still use discretion in their application of the law, but with much less ease. This change has brought both positive and negative consequences. By enforcing the letter of the law, the assumption is that citizens become more law abiding. Lawlessness is less tolerated.

Introduction

The potential negative with the heavy emphasis of the law consistently enforced is that officers are placed in situations that can make them less safe because the citizens and their personal realities are negated, and enforcing the law is all that matters. Citizens become objects and officers become robots in their application of the law.

A second issue is the heavy reliance on the use of the duty belt and the technology associated with it. The use of non-lethal technology (OC spray, electronic control devices, expandable metal batons, etc.) has been far better because it can cut down on physical injury to officers when controlling someone who is resisting arrest. The problem is that some officers will frequently go to the duty belt too quickly when less physical control might also work.

A third issue is that some officers often take a very aggressive approach toward citizens regardless of their behavior. The goal of this approach is to take immediate control. Unfortunately, this approach also causes some citizens to react aggressively to the officer because they feel they are being attacked without cause. A loud voice with aggressive facial display may work with some citizens and not others. It might, in fact, cause an unsafe situation if the situation escalates for example, some citizens could resist the officer.

The goal of this book is to not be negative about the criticality of the duty belt technology or not to take an aggressive approach when needed. The goal of this book is to add to the skills an officer can utilize to manage citizens.

An analogy is the repertoire of a baseball pitcher. A professional pitcher, who has only one type of pitch, such as a fast ball (aggressive), is going to be in trouble because some of the hitters aren't intimidated by it. The smart pitcher has additional types of pitches (curve ball, slider, etc.) in their repertoire and so is more likely to win. By adding social intelligence skills to an officer's repertoire, we are increasing their chances of success in all types of officer-citizen encounters.

The concept of "Community Policing" has been stressed for many years. The concept is good, but unfortunately is not working in some instances because meeting with a citizen, citizen review boards, police explorers, or police youth leagues can help, but the bottom-line is not the above. The bottom-line is the military concept or intelligence agency concept of "Boots on the Ground". The individual actions of every soldier or intelligence operative is the critical key to success regarding community relations.

From a law enforcement perspective, "Boots on the Ground" means every officer has to be equipped with social intelligence to insure the success of community policing. This means officers must have pro-social abilities.

Pro-social abilities are the abilities to engage others without anger or fear. Pro-social officers exhibit nonverbal and verbal communication skills that attract people to them. They rarely are at a loss for words and their nonverbal behaviors display confidence when engaging with others. Those who are not pro-social are described as introverted, insensitive, and difficult to talk to.

Emotions are the most under-studied phenomena in science. Some cultures teach people to freely express their emotions, while others teach the complete suppression of emotions. This probably is due to the fact that emotions are powerful in their influence over us and others.

Emotions are biological in nature. Their primary function is to move us to act or not act in a certain way. They are basically the foundation of what we call motivation; without them, we would appear lifeless.

The problem with emotions is their possible negative influence on our thinking and behavior. People who have lost control will often say, "I don't know where my head was at when I did that." They are referring to the fact that extreme emotions of anger, fear, and sadness control the rational part of your brain to think straight.

Lawful Authority

The next essential step in building confidence is learning and understanding lawful authority. To be a better and more effective communicator, it is essential to learn and understand the lawful authority granted to each officer. Possessing this knowledge and better yet, understanding this authority, will prepare the law enforcement officer to speak not only more intelligently, but with more confidence. Officers need to understand where their authority is derived and what grants them the authority to perform their duties.

Learning as much as possible about the Constitution of the United States of America, its amendments and relevant case law associated, are all very important components of knowing the base of one's lawful authority. It is imperative that officers of the law continuously review and study federal law, state and local law, and case law so that civil rights are not violated. Learning as much as possible about the applicable state constitution, its amendments, and relevant case law associated are also very important. State, county, and municipal law knowledge is essential to building a foundation of knowledge.

Law enforcement officers must know and properly understand what they are permitted to do and not permitted to do in the performance of their duties. Possessing this knowledge is essential to effective communication between officers and citizens.

Knowing and understanding one's lawful authority is also essential to building credibility in a court of law. The actions of officers will constantly be analyzed during their career. Constant review and understanding of case law decisions from higher courts are essential to maintaining credibility in the courts.

(SADA) Safety–Assess–Decide–Action

The acronym SADA (Safety, Assess, Decide, and Action) and learning traits for each portion are introduced in the chapters that follow. All four parts of this acronym apply to the techniques being explained in this book.

Tactical safety is of the utmost importance in any encounter that a law enforcement officer has during the performance of their duties. Officers are taught from the very beginning of basic certification training in the academy how to be safe in everything that they do. Best practices will be reviewed in the next chapter and various scenarios will be provided to further explain how effective communication can take place while still being tactically safe during encounters.

Chapter 2

SAFETY–Assess–Decide–Action

Tactical safety is a component of knowledge in which law enforcement officers must continue to receive annual training. Violence against officers has been on the rise in the United States of America and it is even more important for modern law enforcement officers to understand best practices relating to being tactically safe.

Due to the increased risk of injury to officers, some law enforcement agencies have distanced themselves from defensive tactics training at a time when many agencies are struggling with double-digit (or more) vacancies. Many present-day law enforcement agencies struggle to send officers to attend training because of severe manpower shortages. When officers are able to receive training, it is only the training absolutely required for a job function.

Other law enforcement agencies have placed an emphasis on continued education in the areas of defensive tactics while also incorporating community policing strategies to teach officers how to better interact with the public. One thing is for sure: It is possible for an officer to be tactically safe using best practices while also using techniques and recommendations from this book to more effectively communicate with other people.

It would be impossible to review every possible scenario that a law enforcement officer encounters from day-to-day and make recommendations on how to better improve interactions. Additionally, every situation is different and no call for service, incident, or vehicle accident is the same.

Each call for service involves too many contributing factors to have one set way of having a peaceful and satisfactory resolution for all involved. What is certain, however, is that officers must be safe and keep others around them safe before any possible effective communication can commence.

In the scenarios that follow, six types of calls for service are listed and examples are provided to show how officers worked to ensure a peaceful and satisfactory resolution.

Traffic Stop

Safety is very important on a traffic stop. There is no such thing as a "routine" traffic stop because many factors contribute to what happens during a traffic stop. First and foremost, an officer must be safe. Officers must use the training they received to not only keep themselves safe but to also do their best to ensure the safety of the violator who has been stopped as well as any other people in the immediate area.

Law enforcement academies provide training on how to properly conduct a traffic stop for a violator of traffic laws. There is also continued training provided to officers relating to best practices to use while on the scene of a traffic stop. The first priority is safety of the officer and those who are in the immediate area. It is possible to think and act tactically while also working to more effectively communicate. An example of this is presented in the following scenario.

Making the Point: Traffic Stop

Officer Xavier McGovern, who works in an urban metropolitan city, initiated a traffic stop on a two-lane street. Officer McGovern used all appropriate safety tactics to initiate the stop and his initial approach to the vehicle.

When Officer McGovern began to speak with the driver, he stated: "Hello, I'm Officer McGovern with the Metropolitan Police Department. Would you please provide me with your driver's license? While the driver began to retrieve his driver's license, Officer McGovern stated, "The reason for the traffic stop is because I observed that you were driving with no headlights illuminated. Are you experiencing a mechanical problem with your vehicle tonight?" The driver stated that he was not aware of any problems with his vehicle and added that he just purchased the vehicle and assumed that the lights would automatically illuminate when it was dark enough. The driver added that he didn't even realize the lights were not illuminated and thanked the officer for making him aware.

Officer McGovern, while speaking to the driver using the words and demeanor above, was being both physically tactical *and* socially tactical. He was using all of his senses to ensure that he was keeping himself safe and also doing his best to keep the scene safe. Officer McGovern approached the vehicle in a tactical manner. He stood in a tactical manner in the event that the driver tried to harm him. He watched oncoming traffic often to ensure that there were no threats. He was looking inside of the vehicle for any possible weapons or contraband in plain view. He was using his senses to see or smell any evidence of alcohol or drug use. Officer McGovern was doing what many officers do on a daily basis. He was multi-tasking while attempting to accomplish a goal.

There are many different ways that the above traffic stop conversation could begin and ultimately proceed. The above example offers one of the ways to start a conversation with a traffic violator while showing respect from the very beginning. In doing so, Officer McGovern is showing the violator that he intends to give respect and be transparent about the reason for the traffic stop.

Of course, not every traffic stop will be a perfect scenario as illustrated in the example scenario. Some traffic violators don't even allow an officer to speak the first word before they are shouting out of the window as the officer approaches. The example only provides one way of starting an encounter in a socially tactical way which ultimately leads to a better encounter. Any commander who investigates a complaint or any jury that views the video of this traffic stop would immediately note that the officer was friendly, polite, and transparent from the very first word of the verbal encounter. If the driver had reacted differently and was disorderly, or if the driver was arrested for DUI or some other offense, the officer's social tactics would not come into question if the driver had filed a complaint. As it will be mentioned many times throughout this book, most complaints filed against law enforcement officers are due to the way that the person says they were spoken to while interacting with the officer. Think about how the above traffic stop would have proceeded if Officer McGovern started off the verbal dialogue with only uttering the words, "Driver's license?" The driver more than likely would have reacted much differently and the overall outcome would have been different.

Domestic Violence

Domestic disputes are one of the most dangerous calls for service that a law enforcement officer handles. There are many different contributing factors that make each dispute different. What is common about these disputes however are that two or more human beings are having a conflict in which law enforcement must intervene. There may have been a request for law enforcement to intervene from one of the persons directly involved in the incident, or the officer may have observed or overheard the incident and it was their duty to intervene to maintain peace and order. Regardless, tensions are high among those involved. Emotions are strong and people are often not thinking clearly, which sometimes leads to hasty, impulsive, or dangerous actions. It is imperative that officers are physically safe in their approaches to these incidents. While being physically safe, it is also important to be socially tactical when possible. Officers must use all senses to determine if there is a threat and when they must react to that threat.

With regard to being more socially tactical, the following is an example of an incident illustrating the techniques an officer used to de-escalate a situation.

Making the Point: Domestic Violence Call

Deputy Michelle Ashwood was dispatched to a domestic dispute between an adult male and adult female in an apartment. The female involved in the dispute called 911 and requested that a deputy respond and ask her live-in boyfriend and father of her child to leave the apartment. The female stated that the two have been arguing all day about finances and that the dispute has gotten more heated in the last hour. The female complainant told the 911 operator that her boyfriend had begun throwing items around the residence in anger and that she was afraid for the safety of her 6-year-old son. The female stated that she and her son made an attempt to leave the residence but her boyfriend told her that she had better not try to leave with the child or she would regret it. There are no weapons in the house and the dispute has not been physical to this point.

Prior to Deputy Ashwood's arrival, another deputy arrived on scene of the domestic disturbance and made contact with the two adults involved. Deputy Ashwood arrived in the area and approached the residence as she would any other report of a domestic disturbance. She used all of her senses to evaluate the current state of the situation and remained physically tactical. Upon entering the residence, she observed the other deputy standing in the living room, speaking to an adult male who was sitting on the sofa. The male was very loud and agitated at the deputy who first arrived on scene. Deputy Ashwood observed that the conversation between the deputy and the adult male was very sarcastic and tense. The deputy who arrived on scene first leaned over to Deputy Ashwood and stated, "We're going to have to fight this guy. He's not going to come quietly."

Deputy Ashwood continued to listen to the back-and-forth conversation between the other deputy and the adult male. During the tense exchange of words, Deputy Ashwood made the observation that the other deputy was using words that were escalating the male's attitude and angering the male more and more.

Deputy Ashwood noticed that there was a video game system connected to a television in the living room area. She also noticed some action games lying on the floor next to the game box. She intervened and asked the male if he played the game with his son. The male replied to Deputy Ashwood, "Yes, I play the game with my son. Is that against the law too?" Deputy Ashwood smiled and stated, "No sir, but I have been looking for this particular game to purchase for my son and haven't been able to find it anyplace. Where did you buy it?" The male responded, naming the store. Deputy Ashwood then had about a 1-minute conversation with the male about the game and thanked him for the information.

Deputy Ashwood de-escalated the emotions of the male and built somewhat of a rapport with him. When the other deputy interjected and began speaking about the domestic dispute again, the male interrupted the deputy and told him that he didn't want to talk to him any longer and that he only wanted to talk to Deputy Ashwood because she showed him respect. Deputy Ashwood smiled and took over the questioning related to the incident. She determined that the male needed to be arrested and because she was socially tactical, she was able to get him into custody without incident.

It is not possible to be socially tactical in every domestic dispute situation. Many times, officers encounter people who cannot be deescalated, no matter how many methods an officer tries. The above example illustrates only one way or method that could be used to more effectively communicate with another person while trying to deescalate the person's agitated mood.

Burglary

There are two types of burglary calls that will be reviewed in this section. The in-progress burglary call for service and the burglary report call for service. The in-progress call for service involves a crime that is taking place as the officer arrives on scene. The report call for service involves someone requesting to file a report of a burglary that has occurred in the recent past.

While responding to in-progress burglary calls, it is imperative that the officer focus on the information that is being provided by the dispatcher while also formulating a plan of approach using best practices with regard to being physically safe and tactical. The in-progress burglary call is a very dangerous call for service, and responding officers need to be focused on safety first and foremost. Social tactics may be used when interacting with dispatchers via police radio, when interacting with potential complainants on scene, or when interacting with other officers. The social tactics are to be used in conjunction with defensive tactics and other methods used to be safe while handling the call for service. The effective officer doesn't use voice inflection via the police radio (although it might be difficult at times) and upon arrival on the scene must realize that a complainant who may be present doesn't fully understand law enforcement protocol or terminology. Yet again, law enforcement officers are expected to multi-task in very tense situations and not only keep all people safe, but also apprehend suspects in an objectively reasonable way.

When responding to a burglary call for service in which the burglary has occurred in the recent past, the priority of the call is lowered because there generally is not a potential danger to another person's life. When officers are requested to respond to a burglary that has occurred previously, the encounter is typically with a homeowner or business owner who has suffered a loss of property and been left to feel violated and sometimes scared of a potential further crime. It is important that officers who respond to a call of this nature understand that what might be "just another burglary call" to them may very well be a very traumatic event for the victim. The victim wants to feel that they are being treated with dignity and respect while also feeling that this crime will be investigated using all resources available.

Sometimes, officers may become frustrated when arriving on scene after learning that victims have moved items, touched items, or inadvertently moved, cleaned, or disposed of valuable evidence prior to the officer's arrival. Again, it is important for the officer to realize that what might be "common sense" to them might not be "common" to the non-law enforcement minded victim. With this in mind, an officer should use social tactics when communicating with complainants and not belittle or insult. The example provided below illustrates one way to be socially tactical.

Making the Point: Burglary Call

Officer Donny Smith was dispatched to a report of a burglary that had occurred previously at a house located within a neighborhood. While driving to the location, the dispatcher advised via police radio that the owner of the home had just returned from a one-week business trip and found that his home had been burglarized. The dispatcher further stated that the complainant had walked through the residence and stated that the suspect(s) were no longer present.

Officer Smith arrived and made contact with an adult male, adult female, and two teenage kids in the driveway of the residence. He took note of the complainant's name (John Hastings) on his in-car computer screen prior to exiting his vehicle. As he walked up to the group standing in the driveway, he stated, "Hello, I am Officer Smith with the Wayside Police Department." While looking at the adult male in the group, he further stated, "Are you John Hastings?"

The male replied, "Yes." Officer Smith then proceeded to explain what he was informed by the dispatcher and confirmed that no suspects were present within the residence. John confirms that he walked through the entire residence and is absolutely certain that no one was inside.

At this time, John's cellular phone rang and he stated that the person calling was his insurance agent and he needed to take the call. John told his wife to "talk to the cop while I handle this." Officer Smith asked the wife of John Hastings to explain what happened.

Mrs. Hastings said that she was "just in shock." She stated that she and the kids arrived home about one hour earlier from running a few errands. She said that when they arrived home, John met them in the driveway and stated that the house had been burglarized. She said that John told her that there were a lot of things missing, but would not allow her or the kids to go inside until the police arrived. She said that he told her the back door was kicked in and there was a lot of stuff missing. Mrs. Hastings stated, "that's all I know; you'll have to talk to John for more information."

John was still on the phone with his insurance agent after Officer Smith had completed gathering all available information possible. He then motioned to John and stated, "Sir, I need to speak to you prior to leaving." John stated, "I'll be off the phone soon." At this point, Officer Smith had already completed all work that could be done and needed to get more information from John prior to being able to leave the call for service. There were also calls pending in Officer Smith's zone and he felt a sense of urgency in getting back in service to answer those pending calls for service.

Officer Smith politely walked up to John again. John was frustrated with being interrupted again and asked Officer Smith, "What's so important…I said I would be off soon!"

Officer Smith replied, "I understand that you are frustrated with the many things happening right now. However, I cannot complete this incident report without getting more information from you that is essential to the report. I must go in service as soon as possible because there are other calls for service pending. If you can't answer my questions now, the report cannot be completed in a timely manner, which will delay you being able to retrieve a copy."

John apologized and stated that he was so upset about what happened and did not mean to be offensive. John then provided all needed information to Officer Smith.

In the above scenario, it would have been very easy for Officer Smith to snap back at John when John was rude to him. However, having empathy was important in this situation. Had Officer Smith replied with something harsh, he would have most certainly created hostility which might have ultimately led to difficulty in obtaining the additional information needed to complete the incident report. Most officers have encountered people on calls for service who give priority to a phone call. It is important to realize that what is "common sense" to the officer may not be "common sense" to the victim of a crime. By simply explaining why Officer Smith needed John to get off of the phone in this instance, John better understood that although he was traumatized by this burglary, other people in the community needed police response and Officer Smith couldn't help others until John provided the needed information to him.

Armed Robbery

There are two types of armed robbery calls that will be reviewed in this section. The in-progress armed robbery call for service and the armed robbery report call for service. The in-progress call for service involves a crime that is taking place as the officer arrives on scene, and the report call for service involves someone requesting to file a report of an armed robbery that occurred in the recent past.

While responding to in-progress armed robbery calls, it is imperative that the officer focus on the information that is being provided by the dispatcher, while also formulating a plan of approach using best practices with regard to being physically safe and tactical. Responding units must also be focused on direction from supervisors with regard to setting up perimeters and strategically positioning themselves around the incident location. The in-progress armed robbery call is a very dangerous call for service and responding officers need to be focused on safety first and foremost.

Like any in-progress call, social tactics may be used when interacting with dispatchers via police radio, when interacting with potential victims or witnesses on scene, or when interacting with other officers. The social tactics are to be used in conjunction with defensive tactics and other methods to be safe while handling the call for service. The effective officer doesn't use voice inflection via the police radio (although it may be difficult at times) and upon arrival on the scene must realize that a complainant, victim, or witness who may be present doesn't fully understand law enforcement protocol or terminology. Yet again, law enforcement officers are expected to multi-task and to perform their jobs as professionally as possible.

The armed robbery report call for service generally involves an incident that just took place or that took place within the past hour or less. Responding officers should realize that victims and witnesses to the incident will be very upset. When interacting with people directly related to the incident, officers should try to empathize with those people and use patience when questioning them as to what transpired. Patience should also be exercised when interacting with other people in the surrounding area of the crime. An example is provided in the scenario below.

Making the Point: Armed Robbery Call

Deputy Jarvis Wood responded as a back-up unit to an armed robbery that had just occurred at a local convenience store which was situated near three very large shopping centers. The suspect description was provided to responding units from the first unit that arrived on scene. Additionally, responding units were provided with a clothing description, weapon description, and direction of travel. The suspect was on foot when he fled from the location 20 minutes prior.

Deputy Wood searched inside one of the shopping centers for anyone matching the suspect's description. Many other Sheriff's Office units responded to the area to search as well. A citizen motioned for Deputy Wood's attention as they passed one another while driving in the parking lot. Deputy Wood lowered his driver's side window and asked the driver what he needed. The driver responded, "Man, there's a lot of police around here tonight. What's going on?!"

Deputy Wood responded and informed the citizen of the crime that had just taken place. He explained that everyone was okay presently, but there was an armed suspect who deputies were searching for in the area. Deputy Wood provided the citizen with a description of the suspect and told him to "call 911 to report any suspicious activity."

In the above scenario, Deputy Wood used social tactics when stopping and answering the citizen's inquiry about all of the police activity. Deputy Wood chose not to be rude and informed the citizen of the threat in which deputies were trying to locate. Had Deputy Wood stated "no comment" when he was asked, or uttered something insinuating that it was none of the citizen's concern, the citizen would have not only felt disrespected, but might have also observed suspicious activity and did not report it because they weren't aware what had just occurred. Deputy Wood chose to be transparent with the citizen. He didn't divulge every detail of the crime, but merely explained that there was a threat in the area and to call 911 to report any suspicious behavior.

Suspicious Person

Suspicious person calls for service are one of the most common tasks performed by law enforcement officers. Some of these particular calls for service are dispatched and some of these calls for service are initiated by proactive law enforcement patrols. Social tactic skills are used more frequently when interacting with suspicious persons. Generally, the person who is reportedly "suspicious" will state that they have no idea as to why the law enforcement officer has approached or potentially detained them during an encounter. It is imperative that law enforcement officers use defensive tactics *and* social tactics when interacting with suspicious persons. As always, the first priority is to ensure the safety of the officer as well as other people on scene or in the immediate area.

It is also imperative that officers fully understand their lawful authority for the most effective social tactics to be utilized during a suspicious person call for service. Understanding the Fourth Amendment to the United States Constitution and relevant case law from the United States Supreme Court is essential for law enforcement officers to have a lawful and socially tactical encounter with a citizen in the performance of the officer's duties. The following example is provided.

Making the Point: Suspicious Person

Officer Harold Thomas attended roll call at the beginning of the shift. His supervisor informed him and other officers that numerous car dealerships reported that vehicles had been entered during the previous night and that car radios and other vehicle parts had been stolen. The surveillance video from most of the car lots was poor quality due to foggy conditions the night prior. In all, five car dealerships on East Parkway had a total of 24 cars entered between the hours of 01:00 and 05:16 earlier that day. Although surveillance video was not the best quality from each dealership, it appeared that three persons wearing all dark clothing were occupying two dark-colored passenger cars and that this trio were the same people who committed all of the crimes during this time period.

Officer Thomas' shift began at 21:00 and ended at 07:00. He planned to patrol the parking lots of these dealerships and other parking lots between midnight and 07:00. At 05:30, Officer Thomas observed a person standing in front of a Ford Dealership on East Parkway. As he drove up to the male, the male, who had been standing still to this point, noticed Officer Thomas and began walking down the road. Officer Thomas stopped the male and identified himself as Officer Thomas with the Compton Police Department. The male seemed nervous and told Officer Thomas, "I ain't done nothing, officer." Officer Thomas asked the male for identification and the male replied that he just "broke down" and was walking to get help. Officer Thomas explained that he stopped to talk to the male because there had been a large number of vehicles damaged or entered in the parking lot of the dealership recently and asked the male if he knew anything about it. The male replied, "No, I just broke down— like I told you officer. I'm just waiting on my ride."

Officer Thomas asked where the male's vehicle was located and the male told him. Officer Thomas had another officer check the area described and did, in fact, locate a black truck with the hood up and an antifreeze leak. The registration of the vehicle did return to the male and it did appear that the male legitimately had vehicle trouble.

However, while Officer Thomas continued to speak to the male, he offered additional information to the male regarding why he looked suspicious to him. He explained about the timeframe in which the crimes had been committed earlier in the day and mentioned that when he first observed him standing on the roadway, he thought he might have been acting as a lookout for others who might be committing a crime. The male stated that he only stopped because he had a co-worker coming from the factory down the street to pick him up and that he wanted to give him a good place to see him better. The male stated that he began walking when he saw the police car because he was trying to get in a better-lit area to motion for the officer.

As the two continued to speak, the male stated that he works the graveyard shift at the factory down the street and normally goes to take a break between 05:30 and 06:00. He told Officer Thomas that he observed three males inside of the convenience store the morning prior and overheard one of the males in the store telling another male that they "needed to sell the radios as soon as possible."

Officer Thomas collected the descriptions of these males and provided all information to the detectives working the entered auto cases. Due to the social tactics used by Officer Thomas during this incident, detectives were able to gather more information from the convenience store and ultimately make arrests.

Again, not all situations end as the above incident ended. However, knowing his lawful authority, Officer Thomas knew what he could and could not do during this incident. He knew that he had to safely ascertain that this male was not a suspect in the previous cases. But Officer Thomas took this incident further and used social tactics to explain his reasoning for the stop. By doing so, he learned information that ultimately led to the arrest of the suspects that committed the crimes.

School/Workplace Violence

There are many examples in recent decades of how violence in schools and workplaces has become a large problem for law enforcement. Growing concerns over the economy, anger, greed, terrorism, and mental illness are just some of the reasons in which the United States has experienced an increase in incidents of violence. When officers are dispatched to an in-progress violent incident at a school and/or workplace, the stress level is extremely high due to the high probability that many persons could be injured or possibly killed in a very short time if law enforcement intervention doesn't take place promptly. Safety is of the utmost concern for all law enforcement responding to a violent scene—not only safety of the officers but also for all human life.

When responding to a report of an active shooter or some other threat to human life at a workplace or school, the number one essential goal for officers is to stop the threat using knowledge, training, and experience. The training used by most officers generally relates to something physical, such as defensive tactics and/or firearms tactics. Officers arriving to scenes make quick decisions based upon the totality of the circumstances regarding what non-lethal or lethal tactics will be used to have the best possible conclusion. Physical tactics may include the use of defensive tactics, chemical agents to subdue a suspect, electronic control devices, expandable metal batons, or a deadly force weapon.

The intent of this book is to stress the importance of using social tactics, when practical. It is understood that law enforcement officers must use physical tactics, sometimes within seconds of arriving on the scene of a violent crime. The techniques listed in this book offer ways for officers to be professional when situations allow and to use social tactics when it is safe to do so. An example of how these techniques can be used in a school violence situation is provided below.

Making the Point: School/Workplace Violence

Offers were dispatched to a local middle school one afternoon due to a report of a gun being discharged within a restroom. There is limited information provided to the 911 operator and it is unknown who the shooter is, where the suspect might be located, or if anyone is injured. Additionally, the School Resource Officer assigned to the school cannot be reached, but is shown as being present at the school. There are many questions that are present as officers arrive on scene and it takes almost 30 minutes to determine that the scene is safe and that there are no injuries. During this time-frame, the large police presence at the school has the attention of local media and many parents.

It is absolutely necessary that officers use social tactics after determining that there is no longer a threat within the school and that no injuries are reported. There are many different examples of people who need information or feel entitled to information. During an incident of this nature, numerous officers are conducting many different operations that contribute to the overall handling of the incident. Examples include:

- Officers conducting interviews with witnesses/victims;

- Officers communicating with school administration regarding the incident and the release of information to the employees and students contained within the school;

- Officers communicating with parents and other concerned parties outside of the school, providing updates and ensuring everyone that there are no injuries while also being transparent about what is known at the time;

- Officers communicating with angry drivers who are being rerouted due to street closures;

- The general public stopping to ask questions about the incident;

- Media requesting information about the incident; and

- Many different agencies working together to handle the scene (police, sheriff deputies, fire department personnel, EMS personnel, public works personnel, etc.).

It is essential, after there is no longer a threat, for officers to realize that their social skills are now needed to effectively manage the scene until its conclusion. It is essential for officers to use basic knowledge in assessing the scene to decide what action is best depending on what they are encountering at the time.

Chapter 3

Safety–ASSESS–Decide–Action

Sizing up the situation first begins with knowing one's authority, knowing that the authority is legitimate, and also practicing safe tactics. This chapter will focus on proven skills that will improve a law enforcement officer's interaction and ability to communicate with other people.

Sizing up any situation involves five very *basic* skills:

1. Arranging
2. Positioning
3. Posturing
4. Observing
5. Listening

The word "basic" is important here. The five skill areas are basic and fundamental to everything you will learn in Chapters 3 and 4 of this book—and to everything that you will actually do on the job. An officer cannot hope to communicate safely and effectively with a person or persons until they have used these skills to size up a situation.

Arranging

Before "Assessing" can be attempted, one must first practice the skill of arranging. For the purposes of this text, "arranging" is the process of organizing one's self and environment to encourage the most effective communication. Essentially, when an officer arranges their environment, they are utilizing physical tactics.

Law enforcement officers are trained from the very beginning of most basic mandate training curriculums to always be defensive and use good judgement and tactics when performing their daily duties. Using knowledge, training, and experience, it is possible for law enforcement officers to be tactically defensive using approved best practice methods while also applying the techniques listed within this book to more effectively communicate with others and build trust within communities.

In most defensive tactics training classes for law enforcement, officers are taught how to use best practice methods to not only keep themselves safe, but also to ensure the safety of others the officer encounters. Law enforcement officers routinely use defensive tactics in their daily interaction as a part of muscle memory. For example, an officer may stand in a bladed stance when communicating with someone, as they have been trained to keep their weapon side-angled away from the person standing before them. This is necessary when interacting with suspects as the person may be a potential threat.

There are also many interactions that an officer has each day with people who are less likely to be a threat. An example would be an officer who is called to the home of a resident because their vehicle was stolen from their driveway during the night. Upon arrival, the officer arranges the environment by being prepared before making contact with the victim of the vehicle theft. The officer carries any needed materials (notebook, business cards, etc.) as they make the first contact. This eliminates the need to leave the victim's presence while documenting the details for an incident report. After the officer determines that there was not a repossession that took place, the officer begins to ask questions for the purpose of completing the report. During this process, it is likely that the homeowner is not a threat to the officer and the officer could begin arranging the environment to encourage effective communication.

Another way of arranging is to remove any outside distractions. If there is a lot of commotion inside the residence, the victim could be asked to step into another room or to step outside. Simple communication with the victim allows the officer to "arrange" the environment to encourage effective two-way communication so that there are no mistakes made when completing the incident report.

Another example of arranging can be applied to a traffic stop that an officer conducts. An example of this is provided on the following page.

Making the Point: Traffic Stop

Officer Tyrone Swift was patrolling one afternoon on a two-lane roadway in which the posted speed limit is 45 miles per hour. Officer Swift was traveling east and observed a blue passenger car traveling west, towards him, at a high rate of speed. Officer Swift visually estimated that the speed of the blue passenger car was approximately 65 miles per hour and used a speed detection device to check the speed of the approaching vehicle. The speed detection device produced a reading of 67 miles per hour. Officer Swift safely initiated a traffic stop on the blue passenger car and made contact with the driver.

As Officer Swift approached the vehicle, he used good tactical skills and was prepared for any potential threat that might have presented itself. After speaking to the driver and asking for a driver's license, Officer Swift wanted to arrange his environment better because of the passing motorists on this moderately-busy, two-lane roadway. In an effort to arrange effectively, Officer Swift asked the driver to exit the vehicle and step to the rear passenger side. In this process, Officer

Swift communicated with the driver and asked him to place his back toward oncoming traffic while standing on the shoulder of the roadway. By doing this, Officer Swift could communicate with the driver while also monitoring oncoming traffic. This placed both he and the driver in a safer position while Officer Swift completed the traffic stop.

In the above scenario, Officer Swift effectively arranged his environment and attempted to encourage an atmosphere that could create a better encounter between the violator and Officer Swift. Officers often forget that each person who is stopped in a traffic stop more than likely remembers every detail of the encounter and will often tell friends and family about the encounter. It should be every officer's intention to not only perform the duty of enforcing traffic laws, but to also treat the citizen with as much dignity and respect as they will allow. This arranges a scenario that will hopefully allow people stopped on a traffic stop to at least talk about how well they were treated, even though they might not be pleased with receiving a traffic citation.

When assessing, you are essentially using sizing up skills that help you know what is happening in any situation. Sizing up helps you avoid costly mistakes and maximizes the chances that your decisions and actions will be effective and accurate. Sizing up works because it gets you ready to use information to manage and often prevent problems. Assessing is always appropriate because you need to size up every situation.

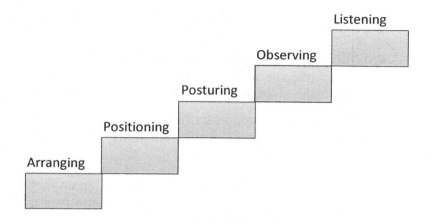

An officer cannot have effective communication unless they have first sized up a situation. On the other hand, by learning to make continual use of these five basic skills, officers can maximize their chances of making the right response in situations where a wrong response could be very costly.

The five basic skills are cumulative in that each new skill builds on each previous one. For example, posturing yourself effectively means that you should already be in an effective position; observing accurately means that you should be in an effective position and posture. Once you are in an effective position and postured in order to observe accurately, you are ready to listen. In other words, you don't simply use one skill at a time. Instead, you size up a situation by making maximum possible use of all five basic skills.

In general, of course, the skilled law enforcement officer always systematically sizes things up during a work day, whether working in traffic enforcement, responding to calls for service, or working a special detail or event. Here are some ways a law enforcement officer sizes things up during a tour of duty:

- Officers meet face-to-face with victims and witnesses of crimes numerous times each day;

- Officers interact with people suspected of committing a crime and must be physically tactical for safety while using all of their senses to perform their duties;

- Officers are engaged in traffic enforcement and must interact with citizens while remaining tactical and cognizant of safety concerns.

During a tour of duty, officers are constantly sizing up their surroundings. Officers instinctively position themselves in a certain way and posture themselves in a manner that is most appropriate for the situation in which they are engaged. Of course, all officers observe and listen to numerous people each day. But how effective is the patrol officer while performing these functions? What perception does the officer portray when communicating with people in the performance of their duties? Nothing in this text should imply that officers are to not remain tactical when engaged in officer-citizen encounters.

It is imperative that officers use common sense (which is common to them) when applying the intervention skills model to their interactions. But, what is "common sense?" To completely understand the term "common sense", it is necessary to define each word.

The word "common" essentially refers to a behavior or task that is completed in a certain way by a certain person or group of people that have similarities. For example, it is common for some law enforcement officers to tell one another to "stay safe" when leaving the presence of another law enforcement officer. This essentially is their way of saying goodbye to, or leaving the presence of a person in which they share similarities.

The word "sense" means to be aware or to understand. For example, officers have the sense to know that officer safety and the safety of all citizens is most important when communicating with suspects in the field, which would require them to often have a tactical or cautious approach when communicating with people in the performance of their duties. Officer safety is always of the utmost importance and it should be noted that using the intervention model can be accomplished in most situations regardless of severity. Sometimes, tensions are high in incidents and officers must immediately react to whatever threat is present. In situations where following the intervention skills model is not feasible, the officer should, at a minimum, maintain the procedural justice mindset.

Essentially, when one uses the term "common sense", it needs to be understood what might be common to one person might not be common to another person.

Positioning

Positioning means putting yourself in the best possible place to observe, hear, and listen; to see and hear individuals or groups. This helps you see and hear what you need to in order to carry out your duties, protect yourself, and keep minor incidents from becoming major ones.

The three parts of positioning are: distancing, facing squarely, and looking directly.

Physically positioning yourself in relation to an individual or group is very important when communicating. The difficult task is positioning yourself properly, given the many unique and difficult scenarios that law enforcement officers face each day on each contact with another person.

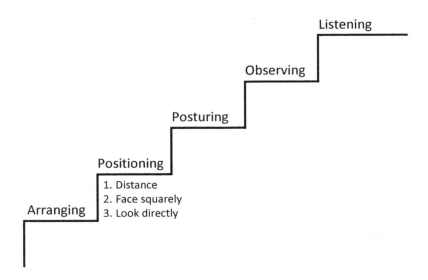

There are several different principles or activities that you might feel are important to effective positioning. The three basic parts of positioning that are the focus in this chapter are establishing an appropriate distance, facing squarely, and looking directly.

As an effective law enforcement officer, you need to position yourself where you can see and hear problems. Being in a good position helps you to recognize a potential problem and, therefore, de-escalate the problem quickly or to come to a suitable solution. Not all interactions are with suspects and others who might present a threat. Officers have interactions with co-workers, supervisors, court personnel, and other professionals during the course of a normal day. Effectively positioning during a conversation allows for better listening and a better response. The more you use positioning skills to see and hear, the less likely it is that the other party will lose interest in the conversation or become distracted. The other party will feel as though they had your complete attention and that you cared about the topic being discussed. The three specific skills of positioning allow for the beginning of effective communication.

THE FIRST PART OF POSITIONING

Distancing. The first principle of distancing is to be able to observe and listen. First, determine what safety level your interaction requires. Proper distance between you and the other person or people with whom you are communicating is essential to being an effective listener and responding appropriately. Always have the mindset that you want to project an image of care and concern to a person or people you are speaking to. When properly distancing yourself, always remember to have a safe and comfortable distance while also remaining effective. Of course there will be many situations where you cannot observe someone; for example, talking via telephone or police radio. In situations such as these, other methods, which will be discussed later in this book, will guide you to maintaining effective communication.

THE SECOND PART OF POSITIONING

Facing squarely. Facing squarely, or fully, ensures that your position gives you the most effective line of vision. Your left shoulder should be lined up with the left boundary line of the area you are watching and your right shoulder should be lined up with the right boundary line of the area you are watching. When you move your head to either side so that your chin is right above either shoulder, you should be able to see the entire field for which you are responsible.

Sometimes the size of the area for which you are responsible (for example, a section of a community) makes it impossible to remain in one position. In this situation, you must rotate yourself so that by successful movements, you will squarely face all of the areas or people you are responsible for observing. Facing fully helps you to size up a situation. You can see best when you directly face people. When your goal is communicating with people (Section II), this also lets them know that you are open to hearing them.

Of course, if safety is an issue, then you would not face a person or situation that exposes you to physical harm or danger.

THE THIRD PART OF POSITIONING

Looking directly. When positioning yourself, you should look directly at the area or person(s) in which you are communicating. Unless you look directly, you will not be on top of the situation even if you are in the right position and facing squarely. Looking directly at a person or group of people often involves looking at their eyes. When questioning people, for example, you will be able to get important clues by observing their eyes and their facial expressions closely.

In addition to the information you can get, your direct look tells people that you are confident and not threatened. This doesn't mean you get involved in a staring contest. But many people believe that a person who won't look you in the eye is being deceptive.

Eye contact may also be the best way of communicating interest. People become aware of our efforts to make contact with them when they see us looking directly at their faces. Of course, looking directly at people will also provide you with valuable information about them. People who keep shifting their eyes while talking to you signal that, at the very least, they are uncomfortable with you or with what is being said. This kind of information is important in law enforcement.

You must also keep in mind that "direct" eye contact may be threatening to some people based on the individual or circumstances (cultural differences).

Making the Point: Sizing Up

Lieutenant Baker is the shift commander for B Squad. She has two Sergeants who supervise the squad. Lieutenant Baker's primary responsibilities involve administrative work such as approving incident and accident reports, coordinating the squad schedule, handling requests for time off and training time, and any disciplinary issues that might arise.

Sergeant Jones is one of the two Sergeants who report directly to Lieutenant Baker. Sergeant Jones needs to discuss a personnel matter with Lieutenant Baker and decides to go to her office one day during the shift. After knocking and being told to enter, Lieutenant Baker asks Sergeant Jones, "What's up?" Sergeant Jones begins talking to Lieutenant Baker, who is facing her computer and actively typing on the keyboard. Lieutenant Baker never stops typing and appears to be pausing while typing as if she is contemplating what to type next. Sergeant Jones immediately gets the impression that Lieutenant Baker's priority is her work on the computer and not on him. He decides to pause and wait for Lieutenant Baker to finish her work on the computer. Lieutenant Baker tells him, "Go ahead, I'm listening."

In this scenario, Lieutenant Baker is not physically positioned appropriately to have effective communication. She, perhaps not intentionally, is showing Sergeant Jones that his needs are not her priority at the moment. If she wanted to have a more effective conversation with Sergeant Jones, she would stop her work on the computer and turn to face Sergeant Jones while asking what he needed. Perhaps standing and making eye contact while asking Sergeant Jones what he needed would display even more care and concern.

Additionally, after learning that the discussion involved a personnel matter that might take a few minutes to discuss, Lieutenant Baker could eliminate the barrier of her desk being between the two and walk around to sit beside Sergeant Jones while discussing the matter. By sitting beside Sergeant Jones and facing him squarely, Lieutenant Baker is sending a very clear message that Sergeant Jones and his concerns have her complete and full attention. It is very important to eliminate distractions when interacting with another person, but this will be addressed later in this book.

Posturing

Using good posture means holding your body in a way that shows strength, confidence, interest, and control. When you appear strong and confident, people will believe that you are strong and confident.

The three parts of Posturing are: standing/sitting erect, eliminating distracting behaviors, and inclining slightly forward.

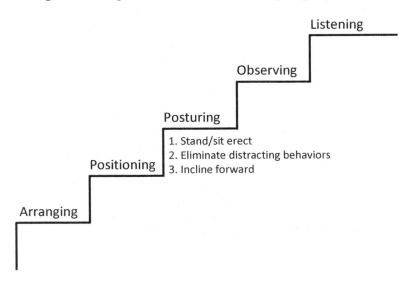

Your posture—how you carry yourself—tells people a lot. It can make a person believe that you are confident in yourself or that you are really pretty worried about what might happen. Your aim, of course, should be to show your real confidence.

As with positioning, there are several ways in which you can use posturing when you are sizing up a situation. Here, we will focus on the three specific procedures of standing/sitting erect, eliminating distracting behaviors, and inclining yourself forward.

The way in which the first two procedures show confidence should be obvious. When you stand or sit erect and get rid of distracting behaviors, you let people know that you are in full physical control—control not only of your body but of the whole situation. This is essential!

Many people will try to intimidate any law enforcement officer who doesn't look as if they are confident about what they are doing. If a person thinks they can intimidate you, you are in real trouble. Any officer who does not have the respect of co-workers or citizens is open to embarrassment and abuse. For example, an officer who lacks knowledge on recent law changes or policy and procedure revisions will almost always result in that same officer lacking confidence in him- or herself. This lack of confidence might cause the officer to present body language indicative of lacking confidence. The ultimate result is an officer who citizens and co-workers do not trust and could be a liability to the agency. By standing erect and eliminating distracting behaviors, you show your strength and that you mean business.

It is imperative to eliminate distracting behaviors when communicating effectively with another person or with a group of people. Using electronic devices, chewing or smacking gum, and tobacco use are just a few of the examples of distracting behaviors that could cause communication to be ineffective.

The third part of the posturing skills outlined here, inclining yourself forward, can also show confidence by reinforcing the idea that all your attention and potential energy is committed to job performance. Inclining yourself forward can also help you communicate your interest when you choose to provide any human service. Used in this way, such a posture says to another person, "I am inclined to listen, to pay attention, to be interested, to help."

THE FIRST PART OF POSTURING

Standing/sitting erect. Everyone understands how important erect posture is, especially to presenting positive and interested body language. You probably heard it as a child, and you definitely heard it if you were in the armed services: "Stand your full height;" "Be proud, stand up straight;" "Stick out that chest;" and "Pull in that gut."

Erect posture takes muscle tone and practice. Look in the mirror and check yourself out. Are your shoulders straight? Is your chest caved in? How do you feel? Ask someone else for their reaction. Posturing means standing or sitting erect to show strength and confidence.

THE SECOND PART OF POSTURING

Eliminating distracting behaviors. A person who cannot stand steady is seen as not at ease with him- or herself or others. Biting nails, foot-tapping, and other distracting behaviors do not communicate confidence and control. But standing stiff like a board does not communicate it either. You should not feel tension in your body after eliminating distracting behaviors.

Other distracting behaviors include anything that might send a message to the other person that some other task is more important than the conversation taking place at the present time. For example, using a cellular phone in any manner (texting, utilizing emails, answering a phone call) while communicating with someone face-to-face, sends the message that the device is more important than the conversation taking place. Posturing means eliminating all distracting behaviors.

THE THIRD PART OF POSTURING

Inclining forward. Your intention here must be to communicate interest and concern by shifting your weight forward so that people become more aware of your "inclination" to communicate with them and show respect. This does communicate "moving closer" without actually moving you much closer or making any physical contact. Since this position shows you to be more alert, it also gives you more control over the situation. Lean your weight away from another person. What do experience? Probably a "laid-back" sort of remoteness. You are simply not as involved. Posturing means inclining yourself forward to show that your attention is really focused.

Officers are encouraged to give thought to situations in the past when they have observed other officers (or themselves) in the performance of official duties. Officers, for the most part, predictably performed their duties effectively and were able to accomplish the goal of a peaceful resolution. However, were there times where officers displayed distracting behaviors?

Making the Point: Posturing

A motor vehicle accident involving two vehicles just occurred on a major roadway during rush hour traffic. The two vehicles were damaged to the point that they could not be moved from the roadway without the assistance of a tow truck. The police were called and told that this accident was obstructing the flow of traffic. Officer Smith was dispatched to the traffic accident and told via police radio of all reported details relating to the accident.

Officer Smith arrived on the scene and observed two passenger cars damaged to the point that a tow truck would be needed to assist in removing the vehicles. He also observed people standing near the two vehicles in the roadway and major traffic congestion as cars attempted to maneuver around the accident scene. He exited his patrol unit slowly, with no sense of urgency, walked toward the accident scene and, in doing so, heard a passing motorist call out his name. He stopped and began talking to the motorist, who is a friend of his, about the football game that was on television the night prior. They had to talk loudly because of all the congestion and the people involved in the accident could overhear the conversation. After about 30 seconds, which appears to be a lifetime for those involved in the accident, Officer Smith walked up to the accident scene, leaned up against one of the damaged vehicles, slouched, folded his arms, and stated, "Alright, someone tell me what happened." As one of the drivers began to talk, Officer Smith interrupted the driver, stating, "Wait a minute, I left my notebook in my car. I'll be right back."

In this scenario, Officer Smith showed a lack of concern through his body language and demeanor. To the people involved in the traffic accident, this accident was a very big deal; they are devastated about the damage to their vehicles. Additionally, the stress level was elevated significantly for each driver because they are a traffic obstruction, which prevents traffic from flowing as usual. Officer Smith showed, through his body language and demeanor, that he was not concerned. His slow movements, stopping to have a conversation with a friend, being unprepared to collect information from the drivers, and leaning against one of the damaged vehicles while folding his arms showed signs of a lack of interest or concern. The demeanor displayed by Officer Smith only encouraged frustration and anger on the part of the drivers, which, in turn, could have resulted in verbal or possibly a physical confrontation. Additionally, the frustration from each driver will most likely result in a complaint being filed against Officer Smith.

For Officer Smith to have handled this situation better and more effectively, he should have arrived to the scene, exited his vehicle with all required items to collect information from the drivers, and walked swiftly to meet with each driver. While walking toward the accident scene from his patrol unit, Officer Smith should have greeted his friend who was passing by, but informed him that he could not talk because he was actively working to clear the roadway. Any true friend would understand.

Upon walking up to both drivers, Officer Smith could have shown concern by quickly introducing himself and asking if there were any injuries to confirm what he was told by his dispatcher. Officer Smith could then confirm that each vehicle could not be moved from the roadway and called for a tow truck. Then, he could have asked both drivers to step to the sidewalk, out of the traffic congestion, while beginning to collect information related to the traffic accident. While collecting this information, Officer Smith could have shown true care and concern by facing each driver, making eye contact, and responding in an audible and physical manner such as verbally confirming information and shaking his head in an up and down motion signifying that he understood what each driver was telling him. Additionally, Officer Smith being organized and ensuring that both drivers had voice during this encounter, would better enhance the possibility of effective communication in this scenario.

Observing

Observing is the ability to notice and understand the appearances, behavior, and environment of individuals and groups. Careful observation of actions will tell you most of what you need to know about people, their feelings, and their difficulties. This is one of the most, if not *the* most, frequent task performed by law enforcement officers each day.

The four steps in Observing are: looking carefully, making inferences, determining whether things are normal or abnormal, and deciding if there is trouble or no trouble.

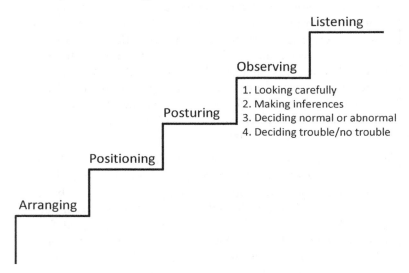

THE FIRST PART OF OBSERVING

Looking carefully at behavior, appearance, and environment. A "behavior" is a nonverbal cue provided by something that a person does while conscious and active. For example, you might observe any or all of the following behaviors: two people holding hands; one person bumping another; a person looking in a store window; a person wringing her hands.

An "appearance" is a nonverbal cue that a person might display even if they were unconscious or dead. For example, you might observe the following appearances: one person has long, brown hair, another didn't wear clean clothes today; a third person is an older person; a fourth person is wearing a t-shirt and shorts.

Environment is the physical settings where people live—neighborhoods, homes, workplace; and the people they live with and relate to: friends, family, and co-workers. It also includes environmental experiences that influence their lives: education, military, and culture.

How does a person look? Where is the person? Who is the person with? When observing a person, you should try to answer mental questions like "What is he doing right now?" (behavior), "What are the important things about how he looks?" (appearance), and "What is important about where he is and who he's with?" (environment). For example, a person commits the offense of speeding when driving faster than the posted speed limit because they are late for work (behavior). An officer's uniform is wrinkled and hair disheveled (appearance) and is separated from his wife and three children living in an apartment alone (environment). Observing means looking at behavior, appearances, and environment. Once you are able to answer these questions, you are ready to draw some inferences about a person. Law enforcement officers constantly use observing skills to assess situations they have encountered.

Making the Point: Observing

> During a 12-hour shift, Deputy Brown observed many people and took mental note of each of their appearances. She observed physical attributes about people such as height, weight, hair color, or potential handicaps. Deputy Brown also took note of behaviors displayed by people, especially when she was requested to handle a call for service. Numerous times during a shift, she observed the behaviors of victims, witnesses, suspects, or innocent bystanders on traffic accident scenes, disputes, thefts, burglaries, and many other types of calls for service. Additionally, Deputy Brown constantly takes note of how the environment looks each time she makes an observation. She frequently makes decisions in her mind as to whether the environment matches or has been affected by what was reported or what she observed once on scene.

THE SECOND PART OF OBSERVING

Making inferences about feelings, relationships, energy level, and values. Inferences are the initial conclusions you come to as the result of observing people. You take in visual cues related to a person's appearance, behavior, and environment. These cues are really "clues" that show you something about a person's feelings, relationships, energy levels, and values. The more observations you make, the more inferences you can draw—and the more accurate these inferences will be. Inferences are important because they provide valuable information that increase your ability to observe another person or predict that person's future behavior. For example, in a domestic situation, a husband may be feeling "down" (feeling) due to his separation from his wife and children (relationship) and his poor grooming may be due to low motivation (energy) because of not seeing his children (values being a parent). Observing means making inferences about feelings, relationships, energy levels, and values.

Making inferences about feelings. Is a person positive, negative, or neutral about others? The officer can use his or her observing skills to draw inferences about how an individual or an entire group of people is feeling. Knowing how a person is feeling is critical in determining where that person really is. For example, you might use the feeling word "happy" to describe a person who is exercising and smiling. For a person who is pacing while wiping his brow, you might apply the feeling word "tense." You might use the term "uptight" to describe a group of people who are tightly clustered and speaking with each other in a well-guarded, hesitant manner.

Making inferences about relationships. Aside from being aware of the nonverbal cues that indicate the feelings of a person, an officer can further increase their effectiveness by looking for cues that indicate the nature of their relationship with the people with whom they work, and with people in general. The relationship between officers and the general population serves as a good indicator of future action.

An officer who has a good relationship with a citizen might gain compliance or come to a peaceful resolution without difficulty or conflict. Conversely, one who has a poor relationship with a citizen might encounter immediate difficulty with just their mere presence. Example: In general, you can categorize relationships and feelings as positive, negative, or neutral. People who do things to make your job easier (e.g., immediately complying with lawful requests) probably have or want to have a positive relationship with you. A person who always tries to hassle you (e.g., uses abusive language, refuses to obey lawful commands) does not have or does not want to have a positive relationship with you. When a relationship is neutral, it is purely business, with no emotional component, positive or negative (for example, a business transaction in a store).

Among people, relationships of power are critical. It is common for people to form their own group with a leader. Knowing the relationship within and between groups is crucial. For example, a group of officers working a certain zone go out together after work. One of the supervisees within the group has had a couple of run-ins with you. He is also the informal leader of the group. You begin to notice that some of the officers in his group are now acting differently with you. This situation could obviously affect your ability to supervise the other officers if you start to have a negative relationship with them.

Making inferences about energy level. Energy level tells us a great deal about how much and what type of trouble a person can or might cause. For example, people with low energy levels are reluctant to initiate anything. This applies to officers and citizens alike. They look and act defeated. Their movements are slow, their heads hang down, and every move seems like an effort. These individuals might spend a good part of their time being non-productive. People with moderate energy levels actively engage in most activities (playing, working, talking, eating) while high energy persons not only participate in all that is required but also make use of physical fitness programs and many other activities. The danger of high energy, of course, is that this energy needs to be used constructively so that it does not become a source of problems.

While it is important to observe basic levels of energy, changes in energy level are even more critical. Energy levels are usually constant for people, except at special times (weekends, special sporting events, holidays). Abrupt changes from high to low and then to high may indicate trouble (to self or others).

It is also important to understand as much as possible about a person's values. Here is where observing the environment comes in. Every person has three basic environments: the place where they live, the place where they work, and the place where they learn. In each of these settings, the actual "environment" will include not only physical materials but people—the people a person "hangs" with. You can learn a great deal about a person by carefully observing their environment. A general rule is: what a person gives their energy to is of value to them; the more energy given, the higher the value.

Values are the ideas (religious beliefs), things (automobiles, jewelry), and people (spouse, children) a person has a strong bond toward.

Knowing what a person values has real implications for effective officers. It is obvious that an officer cannot know everyone within a beat or zone in which the officer may be assigned. However, frequently assigning a specific beat or an area to an officer is actually beneficial to building relationships and trust within a community. If an officer initiates contact with citizens on a frequent basis, it allows the officer to meet and learn more about the people who make up a community or neighborhood. Average citizens are often reluctant to approach law enforcement officers in the field for various reasons, but mainly because they do not want to disturb work that the officer may be doing. Additionally, citizens generally have the idea that they do not need to initiate contact with law enforcement officers if they have not been the victim or witness of a crime. It is incumbent upon law enforcement officers to bridge this gap and to initiate contact with citizens every opportunity that presents itself. Exchanging pleasantries with citizens while walking in a store; stopping to talk with kids in a neighborhood who are riding skateboards and expressing interest in the sport; volunteering to assist with coaching duties at a local school; or joining clubs/groups in the community are all ways in which officers can learn more about the people in their community and also allow the community to learn more about them.

The reasons for your inferences should be visual cues related to behaviors, appearances and environment. Inferences stand the best chance of being accurate if they are based on detailed and concrete observations rather than on vague and general ones (e.g., black hair, scar on cheek, shaking their fist, with three other males in locker room).

Making the Point: Making Inferences

Officer Peterson works the shift from 6 a.m. to 6 p.m. At approximately 3 p.m., he was dispatched to a domestic disturbance where a female complainant alleged that her husband struck her in the face. Both parties were still on scene when Officer Peterson arrived. After ensuring that the scene was safe, Officer Peterson and another officer began to investigate the female's complaint.

Officer Peterson observed that the female's appearance was not normal for most people at 3 p.m. in the afternoon. She was wearing a pink robe and appeared that she had not groomed herself on this date. The female was cursing and yelling, which caused Officer Peterson to have difficulty in determining what transpired between the female and her husband. The husband was with another officer, standing outside in the yard. Officer Peterson observed that the husband was dressed in business-casual attire and appeared to be calm and non-animated. The female would not stop yelling while talking to Officer Peterson and insisted on talking loudly so that her husband could hear her from outside tell

Officer Peterson how worthless he is and how sick and tired she is of the marriage. The female was more focused on criticizing her husband, calling him names and discussing their marital problems, more than she was focused on answering Officer Peterson's questions about the alleged incident that prompted the police being called to the residence.

Officer Peterson looked carefully at the appearance and behavior of the female. He also looked at the environment (the household). Officer Peterson spoke with the other officer on scene and they discussed how to proceed with the call for service. The officers concluded that there was no evidence to support that any physical contact took place and that the female had not taken her medication as prescribed for depression and bipolar disorder.

What was first reported as a domestic disturbance, where a husband had struck his wife, concluded with the officers on scene using observing and interviewing skills to determine the true story.

THE THIRD PART OF OBSERVING

Deciding whether things are normal or abnormal for a given person or persons. Once you have been on the job for some time, you get to know how individuals tend to function through observation. One person is easy-going and hardly ever hassles you or others. Another always looks like they are mad at the world. A third always seems to be feeling depressed. Your observations and the inferences you have drawn can help you determine whether a particular person is in a "normal" or "abnormal" condition for them at any point in time. Observing means determining if things are normal or abnormal.

In determining whether things are normal or abnormal for a person or group at a given time, compare your present observations with any past ones and/or with any comments that other officers might have made about these people. For example, you might observe an individual arguing loudly with another person. He might even be making threats of one kind or another. If this is normal behavior for this person, you probably need to exercise only the usual amount of caution. But if the appearance and behavior of the angry person is highly unusual or abnormal for him, you will know it is a potentially troublesome situation. Example: Consider the fellow officer who is separated from his wife and three children mentioned previously. Normal behavior for this officer is to smile when you initially see him and be very animated (using his hands while talking). His normal appearance is very neat: his hair is neatly combed, he appears to bathe regularly, and his uniform is pressed, creased perfectly, with shoes polished. Since separating from his wife and children (environment), his behavior and appearance has changed; he does not smile very much, is no longer animated, and his uniform and shoes are not kept up.

Making the Point: Normal or Abnormal?

> Officer Warren is a rookie officer that completed the field training program within the past week. He is new to the night shift and completed most of his field training on the day shift. As he was patrolling one day around sunset, he observed a male walking on the sidewalk of a two-lane city street. This male was wearing an American flag as a skirt, a white t-shirt, and a sombrero. As soon as Officer Warren observed the male, he formed the assumption that the male was intoxicated based on his appearance. As he drove closer to the male, he could hear him singing but could not decipher the words due to the high-pitched tone and other factors.
>
> Officer Warren exited his patrol vehicle after notifying dispatch that he was out on a person who was intoxicated in public. Other officers working the shift hear Officer Warren's call and respond to assist him. Upon arrival of a backup unit,

Officer Warren was told that this person is Brian Harris. The backup officer informed Officer Warren that Brian is a veteran who suffers from mental illness. Officer Warren learned from the other officer that Brian sometimes misses doses of his medication, which causes him to wander from his home. The officer had assisted Brian in the past and told Officer Warren that he would take over the call and ensure that Brian got home safely.

Officer Warren learned that although this appearance and behavior was not normal, his first assumption that Brian was intoxicated was incorrect. Using the first, second, and third parts of Observing, and of course the assistance of the other officer, helped this situation to have a peaceful ending.

Later in the evening, Officer Warren met with his supervisor to review the calls he responded to on this date. The discussion of the call involving Brian came up and the supervisor ensured that Officer Warren knew that officer safety was the first and main concern. But the supervisor also taught Officer Warren how appearances and behaviors might not always be what they seem.

THE FOURTH PART OF OBSERVING

Deciding if there is trouble or no trouble. This decision should be based on your observations and your knowledge of the person or persons. With your knowledge of a person, you should be able to generate certain principles that will be useful in making this decision despite "abrupt and/or major changes in behavior and/or appearance that could mean trouble." "An officer who has a history of being positive has a greater likelihood of managing stressful events in life despite changes in behavior and appearance." Observing means deciding whether it is a "trouble" or "no trouble" situation.

Observing appearance and behavior is usually the quickest and most accurate way to detect whether or not a given individual is really having a problem. People may be very reluctant to talk to you about problems. Your observations will allow you to anticipate problems so that you can prepare for their possible impact on other people, on you, other officers, or the person him- or herself. Remember, nonverbal behavior accounts for 65 percent to 90 percent of any spoken message.

Summary for Observing

Law enforcement officers observe many things on a daily basis and numerous times throughout their shifts. A productive officer working a shift will meet dozens of new people each work day and have countless encounters that differ in many ways.

It is important to understand that "observing" is more than what one may physically see with their eyes. Observing with regard to law enforcement involves looking carefully at all surroundings and the behavior displayed by each person. Looking carefully essentially involves how a person might be reacting to situations, the body language they are displaying, and making inferences about individuals. It is important not to stereotype, however, as assumptions about a person's outer appearance may not be accurate.

To accurately observe while working as a law enforcement officer, officers must use all senses to form opinions or conclusions based upon the situation. An example of this would be a domestic violence call for service. Upon arrival to the scene, the officer would strategically and tactfully approach while listening and looking for signs of people engaged in an argument or physical altercation. Officers would use their sense of smell and hearing to determine if any weapons were involved or if there were multiple people involved. Through verbal communication, the officers would ascertain what was normal or abnormal about the scene, the relationship of all parties involved, and what was done to whom during the incident. Essentially, the officer would observe to determine if the incident involved "trouble" or "no trouble." Of course, a person's behavior or appearance is generally a very good indicator or clue, which might lead to credibility of verbal testimony.

Listening

Listening is the ability to hear and understand what people are really saying. Listening helps you hear the signals from people while things are still at the verbal stage so you can take appropriate action to manage situations before they get out of hand.

The four parts of listening are: suspend judgement, pick out key words, identify intensity, and reflect on mood.

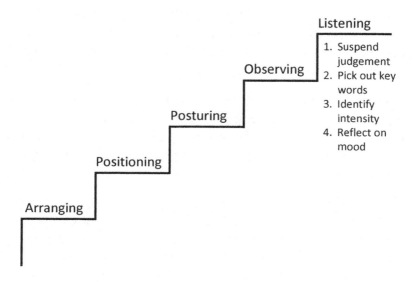

Verbal Cues and Signals

People often go through a verbal stage before the action begins. If you can hear the signals, you can cut off the trouble before it really breaks out. Listening involves your ability to hear and accurately recall all the important verbal cues used by people. It is important because of implied signals of trouble or problems. The danger may be an individual's intention to get into trouble, harm another person, etc.

Complaints are common, of course, but they are also important. An effective officer listens to complaints from citizens and recognizes when a familiar cue is uttered in a new tone— or when a complaint arises from a normal, uncomplaining person. An officer listens especially for changes: silence when there is usually noise or noise when there is usually silence. Once again, the officer asks the question: "Is there trouble here?"

Getting Ready to Listen

As indicated, you should get ready for listening by using the basic positioning, posturing, and observing skills whenever possible. A good position will obviously help you hear better.

Posturing, while perhaps less important in terms of listening for good management, is essential when you are listening to a person who really wants to talk to you. Your posture can signal to the person that you are focusing all your attention on them.

Finally, your observing skills cannot always be used to promote better listening—for example, you might overhear something that people are talking about around the corner. But when possible, visual observations help you to understand the implications of what you're hearing. A person who sounds angry but turns out to be leaning back in his chair and grinning may have only been telling a story to others; an individual whose angry voice fits with his tense, uptight appearance presents quite a different situation.

One more preliminary thing: you cannot listen effectively to people if you have other things on your mind. If you are thinking about home or other job responsibilities, you might miss a lot of what is said and what it really means. You have to focus on the person to whom you are listening—and this takes a good deal of concentration. You can work to develop this kind of concentration by reviewing what you are going to do and who you are going to see before you begin work. Then you will really be ready to start using the four specific procedures that skilled listening involves.

THE FIRST PART OF LISTENING

Suspend judgement. This is very difficult to do for anyone and especially for those in law enforcement. In many circumstances, you have just witnessed a violation of the law. If, however, your goal is to get more information, you will need to get people to open up more. Suspending judgment, at least temporarily, can assist with that. Additionally, always remember that a person's appearance may be deceiving. Do not assume someone lacks education or that they are in any way inadequate based on the way they are dressed.

It is still hard at times to listen without immediately judging because many people with whom you must deal get defensive very quickly when you, as a law enforcement officer, try to talk with them. They might clam up, get upset, or become vague. Despite this, it will severely hurt your efforts if you do not suspend judgment because you will never hear the real verbal cues you need to get more information or to assist someone. Listening means suspending your own judgment temporarily so you can really hear what is being said.

All complaints sound the same after a while—but they are not all the same! Some are just the normal whines and gripes while others are real warning signals of potential problems. Just let the message sink in before making any decisions about it. Of course, certain situations call for quick action, but if you develop your non-judgmental listening ability, you will hear better and be able to take appropriate action more quickly when necessary. A very effective way for a law enforcement officer to begin the listening process when answering a call for service is for the officer to begin the verbal dialogue with the person by asking, "How may I help you today?" When meeting with complainants on a call for service, simply asking this question in the very beginning sends a clear message that you recognize you have been called to serve and protect this citizen and you intend to assist them to the best of your ability.

Making the Point: Suspending Judgement

Officer Boyce has been assigned to a different zone and now walks a foot beat in an area that has recently seen an increase in crime. One day she was dispatched to a construction site where it was reported that two men were arguing. She was told that the complainant's name is Jerry and that he was upset that the construction site was making so much noise near his business.

As Officer Boyce arrived, she observed two men standing face-to-face and talking very loudly. As she approached the two males, she said, "Gentlemen, I am Officer Boyce. Are one of you named Jerry?" One of the men responded saying, "Yea, I'm Jerry." Officer Boyce responded, "Hi Jerry. How may I help you today?" Before Jerry could speak, the other male spoke up and said, "You better get Jerry off my property before I kick his ass!" Officer Boyce responded to the other male stating, "Sir, I am told by my dispatcher that Jerry is the one who called and requested my assistance. But I do want to speak to you as well after I speak to Jerry. Would you please wait here until I return?"

Officer Boyce was not hostile when first walking up to the arguing men. She identified herself and then asked to speak to Jerry. She did not form an assumption as to which of the men were named Jerry. Additionally, when the second man interrupted and stated he was about to physically harm Jerry, Officer Boyce responded in a calm manner, conveying that she intended to give him voice during this encounter after she completed her conversation with Jerry.

THE SECOND PART OF LISTENING

Pick out key words. There are key words and phrases to listen for. Here are a few: "kill," "depressed," "snitch," "moron," "waste," "mad as hell," "I need to hit something." Of course, everything you hear and see must be considered in terms of who did or said it. Some people are always sounding off. In addition to the key words you hear, it is important to add your observations and knowledge of the person who said them. Listening means picking out key phrases such as "mad as hell" or" "kill".

THE THIRD PART OF LISTENING

Identify intensity. Statements are made with varying intensity (high, moderate, and low). The louder and more emotional a statement, the more intense it is. But loudness and emotion are not the same thing. A wavering voice, for example, signals a lot of emotion even though it may not be loud. A statement that is either loud or emotional but not both is most often of moderate intensity.

A statement that is loud and devoid of emotion is usually of low intensity. High intensity statements are very real signs of danger. Listening means determining whether the intensity of a person's speech is high, medium, or low.

THE FOURTH PART OF LISTENING

Reflect on what the mood is. Is the person's mood positive, negative, or neutral? Normal or abnormal? Why? "Mood" here means, at a very simple level, what people are feeling. One question you may ask to determine mood is "What kinds of feelings are being expressed or implied (positive, negative, or neutral)?"

Another question you want to answer is "Is this mood normal or abnormal for this time and place?" Sure, there are always exceptions. For example, a man can say "I'm going to kill you" quietly and without emotion, yet still mean it. This is why it is so important to know as much as possible and to continue to observe and listen for other cues. Listening means determining whether a mood is positive, neutral, or negative, and whether this mood is normal or abnormal.

When you answer the question, "Is this normal or abnormal?" you should try to formulate the reason why this is the case. "Normal" means "as it usually is." This can apply to one person as well as to a large group of people. People are usually quite consistent in their behaviors in their various settings. As we say, "they are creatures of habit." For example, it is not normal for people to be real quiet when they are among others who are being very noisy and animated.

Making the Point: Using Listening Skills

Deputy Edwards is a 7-year veteran of the sheriff's office and has worked in the patrol division since she began her career. She has responded to and handled many different calls for service and is considered to be a productive deputy. She has a reputation for making good decisions while not only being lawful, but building legitimacy with those whom she comes into contact.

Over the course of the past 7 years, Deputy Edwards has been dispatched to investigate a report of rape approximately one dozen times. Out of approximately 12 rape reports that she has handled, only two were legitimate rape cases that resulted in a suspected being charged. The other cases were females that were involved in drugs and/or females that were trying to get attention diverted from something illegal they were doing or something they were doing wrong. Over the years, Deputy Edwards remembers young females alleging rape because their boyfriends got them pregnant by accident and females alleging rape when they exchanged sex for drugs and never received the drugs after performing the sex act. One might say that Deputy Edwards has developed a mindset that reports of rape might generally lead to a false report of a crime.

One evening, Deputy Edwards was dispatched to an apartment to meet with a female who wanted to report a rape. Deputy Edwards responded and while driving to the location, she thought back to the other reports of rape that she had responded to and became angry that she is about to waste her time, yet again, on someone alleging rape. Deputy Edwards arrived and met with the female.

During this call for service, Deputy Edwards told herself that this situation was not similar to the other calls she had responded to in the past. She suspended judgment and gave the female complainant the benefit of the doubt while allowing her to speak. In doing so, she picked up on key words uttered by the female, such as "I have never felt so violated" and "I kept trying to get away. I slapped, punched, dug my nails into his chest and nothing worked; he was just too strong." Deputy Edwards picked out these key words and observed the female's intensity and feeling while explaining what transpired. She quickly knew that this situation was not like the other rape calls she had responded to in the past. As the female continued to speak, Deputy Edwards became empathetic while noticing that the female was trying to keep herself covered with a blanket and seemed ashamed to be seen in this condition.

Deputy Edwards was reminded during this call for service that not all rape cases are false. She was able to use the four parts of listening while also using observing skills to not only handle this case appropriately, but to also show empathy to the victim.

Summary of the Basics

You are an FTO working with a rookie. You are trying to teach him the ins and outs of using basic skills while working in a park. You see the following scene in the park and begin discussing with the rookie: On one bench, two older gentlemen are talking softly—their usual behavior. You have watched them before. They would talk for an hour—no more, no less—all part of their own little routine—no problems. In another place, a young guy is laying on his back in a grassy area. A man beside him, an older man, paces back and forth near him. Tension there; one guy lying quietly, another appearing pretty nervous.

"How's it going?" You stop three or four feet from the older man who turned so that you could face him squarely and at the same time easily observe the younger guy on the ground. "Is that your buddy there on the grass?" "Yeah, he's not feeling so good, so he's getting a snooze in."

The older man nodded and went back to pacing. You turn slightly to get closer to the young guy. Since the older guy still seems nervous, you position yourself so you can keep him in view while you size up the younger man.

Upon closer observation, you notice saliva oozing from the corner of the younger guy's mouth. His lips appeared bluish and you notice that his respiration appeared shallow and erratic. You immediately put in a call for backup and for an emergency medical response. This guy isn't sleeping; he is, in reality, not functioning normally.

All right, you have had a chance to learn the five basic skills you need to size up a situation—to manage your job and people more effectively. You practiced positioning, posturing, observing, and listening. But as you know, there is far more to being an effective officer than being able to size things up. There will be times when you choose to patrol and learn by communicating. You will want to defuse a troublesome situation or get important information. There may even be times you choose to become more involved.

Throughout the sections in this book, the skills you will need to communicate effectively will be reviewed. The skills in this section, while often secondary to other skills in some situations, are absolutely essential when dealing with many tense situations—situations where strong feelings might get out of control or are interfering with your ability to understand what you need to do. Sizing things up just lets you know what is happening and what might happen.

Chapter 4

Safety–Assess–DECIDE–Action

The skill of making a decision using knowledge, training, and experience is a critical job function of law enforcement officers. On every call for service that a law enforcement officer handles, decisions are being made that could affect many different factors and ultimately the outcome of the incident.

Being able to make a decision and effectively communicate will help law enforcement officers open the lines of communication with people. This critical skill provides officers with the ability to get another person to tell more about what they know or think. Officers find that these skills are invaluable whenever they needs to get more information about a situation.

It has been said that the only thing worse than a young person who thinks they know it all is an older person who is sure they know it all—but doesn't. All law enforcement officers have differing levels of life experiences, work related experience, and time on the job. Whatever the situation, there are some officers who are very rigid in their approach. They see little need for juries or judges. To these officers, anything less than making an arrest or charging for every violation is weak and the reason the system does not work.

Although people use their eyes (seeing) and their ears (hearing) all the time, chances are they are never really sure what is going on inside another person's head. At the most fundamental level, people are all human beings and probably much more alike than different, even though it is obvious that criminals are not the same as law enforcement officers. The gulf between an officer and other people may often be frustrating. In one way, the officer feels that they know a person, but in another way, the officer is sure they don't. Knowing other people is important at times. The better an officer understands another person, the more effective the officer can be in terms of communicating with that person.

This is where communication skills become important. When officers choose to use these skills, they can find out a great deal more about the mindset of individuals. Officers can add to their understanding in ways that will help them defuse tension, decrease the chances of trouble, and increase their ability to handle any and all situations more effectively. The basic skills covered in Chapter 3 explain how to size up a situation and asses the situation overall. The communication skills presented in this chapter allow understanding into the full implications of a situation and how to act constructively.

Once an officer chooses to communicate, he or she begins by putting all of the four basic skills to use: positioning, posturing, observing, and listening. As the process of communicating develops, the officer uses new skills in two important ways:

1. Responding to people

2. Asking relevant questions

As the materials that follow make clear, responding to people means a good deal more than just answering a greeting—although this, too, can be important. Officers need to take the initiative in developing effective responses. By the same token, asking relevant questions means more than a simple "Hey, what's going on?"

As noted, communicating must begin with the officer's use of all the basic skills. The officer should position their body at the best possible distance—say three to four feet when talking with a single person (although this would certainly increase if danger was perceived). This puts the officer close enough to see and hear everything, yet not so close that they seem overly threatening. Officers should face the individual squarely, with their left shoulder squared with the other person's right and their right with the other person's left. Officers should look directly at the person, making appropriate eye contact to let them know they are really "right there."

Officers should position their body to communicate both confidence and real attention. Officers need to focus and observe appearance and behavior, using visual cues to draw inferences about feelings and general energy level. Officers should listen carefully, making sure they take in all the key words and verbal indications of intensity so that a person's needs can be determined. Only after officers have really mastered and put to use the basic skills will they be able to use decision making skills effectively.

Like the basic skills, communication skills involve a step-by-step approach. First, the officer must respond to the person. Second, the officer should ask any relevant questions. Then the officer should respond again, this time to the answers. An officer would usually not just jump in and start asking questions—at least not if their goal was to get the person to open up and voluntarily communicate useful information.

Responding

Responding means just that—showing a clear reaction to something that is seen or heard. A response gives evidence that the listener has actually listened. At the simplest level, an officer can respond to content by summarizing and expressing what a person or group of people has said or done. At the next level, officers can respond to the feelings shown in a person's words or reflected in his actions, and the reasons for those feelings.

The three levels of responding are: responding to content, responding to feeling, and responding to feeling and meaning.

Each new level of responding does more to show a person that you are really on top of things, really seeing, hearing, and understanding them. Probably more than anything else in this practice, responding is going to seem strange. It is new and some may be doubtful about its worth. There are some things to remember, however. Officers are not being told that they cannot use other communications techniques that have worked in the past. The intent is to "add-on" to techniques you may already have acquired to increase communication abilities. The more techniques one has to handle a given situation in life, the greater the chances of success or control of the outcome.

THE FIRST PART OF RESPONDING

Responding to content. Responding to content is the skill of seeing and hearing what is really happening and the ability to verbally reflect that understanding back to a person. Officers are letting a person know that they have been heard accurately and are on top of the situation.

While the officer's use of the basic skills establishes a relationship in which people are more likely to cooperate and talk, responding is a tool officers can use spontaneously to communicate with anyone. Responding to content is the first part of effective responding. It shows a person that the officer has heard or seen what they said or did. When people know that you are seeing and/or hearing them accurately, they will tend to talk more freely. This is critical because talking not only provides more of the information needed, it also allows people to get things off their chest.

There are two steps of responding to content: 1) reflecting on what was said, and 2) using the responding format to respond to content.

When responding to content, officers focus on what people are either saying or doing. Officers focus by posturing and positioning their bodies for observing and/or listening to the person.

Next, officers should reflect on what they have seen and heard: "What is he doing?" and "What is he saying?" "How does he look?" In answering these questions, one should stick close to what is actually going on and/or what is being said.

Finally, after taking what has been said and what has been going on and reflecting on it, an officer should summarize what the people are saying or doing. An officer would respond to the content by saying either:

"You look (it looks) _____."
or
"You're saying _____."

(For example, "You look upset" or "You're saying that you're very upset.")

Officers should respond to content when they want more information to aid them. This may occur when they are interrogating or when they notice unusual behavior in a person or group of people and would like to get some information from them about what they are doing. For example, a supervisor might notice a group of unusually talkative officers being very quiet. The supervisor could say to them: "You are all pretty quiet today." This gives the officers the opportunity to respond while also letting them know that you are not only observing them, but observing them accurately. Unlike other approaches designed to get information, responding to content doesn't automatically put people on the defensive.

A typical emotion experienced by citizens when they encounter law enforcement officers can be anxiety. Of course, if you are the citizen who has summoned assistance, the typical impact upon observing the responding officer will be a reduction of your anxiety. Of course, if they think they have done something wrong or they are going to be critiqued by an officer, their anxiety is likely to increase.

When policing people who show signs of anxiety, it is a good idea to let people talk off some of their anxiety rather than for them to act it out. Responding will assist greatly in accomplishing this.

Making the Point: Responding to Content

> You are a patrol officer on the scene of a disturbance involving a male and a female who are considered to be boyfriend and girlfriend. You, as the officer, "position" yourself and are distanced safely, are facing them squarely, and can look directly at them. You "posture" yourself so they know they have your full attention.
>
> You explain to both people that you are there to ascertain what the problem is and that you intend to assist them in resolving their conflict peacefully and to the satisfaction of both. You add that you would prefer that only one person talks at a time. The girlfriend speaks first and states, "He is

always flirting with other women when we are out in public by smiling and winking at them and it is embarrassing to me. He tells me that if I gave him more attention, he wouldn't be flirting so much."

You respond, "So you're telling me that it is your observation that your boyfriend flirts too much with other women in your presence and this behavior makes you uncomfortable." She says, "That's right."

You ask the boyfriend to tell you his side. "Well, I have had other girlfriends in the past who didn't show me enough attention, and that meant that they were seeing someone behind my back. So I figured it wouldn't hurt to show her that I could easily get another girlfriend if I wanted."

You respond, "So you believe that based on your prior experience with other girlfriends that this girlfriend is acting the same way as others have treated you in the past." The boyfriend says, "You got it."

It is important in this situation for the patrol officer to observe both people and their body language, gestures, and reactions while the other person is speaking.

THE SECOND PART OF RESPONDING

Responding to feeling. Responding to feeling is the ability to capture, in words, the specific feeling experience being presented by a person. By responding to or reflecting back the person's feeling, officers show that they understand the feeling. Essentially, one is showing empathy. This encourages the person to talk; to release their feelings.

The two steps in responding to feeling are: 1) reflect on feeling and intensity, and 2) respond to that feeling.

Officers tend to have a warrior mentality and often have difficulty dealing with the emotions of other people as well as their own emotions. Modern best practices encourage officers to have both a warrior mentality and also a guardian mentality. Not properly dealing with emotion is not healthy and leads to other problems. As always, it is recommended that officers be safe, first and foremost, in every situation. However, it is also essential that officers properly handle emotions and the intense feelings that are often associated with them.

Every citizen has feelings that affect what they say and do. The nature and strength of these feelings usually determines what a citizen is going to do. When an officer responds to a citizen's feelings, they are encouraging the citizen to talk. The skill of responding to feelings has important implications for assisting citizens with resolving conflicts or opening up to the officer.

Understanding can defuse bad feelings. When an officer shows that they understand how a citizen feels, that can be more powerful to the citizen than the officer showing that they understand the content of the citizen's actions and/or words. When a citizen feels that an officer understands their negative feelings, those negative feelings can usually be defused. By responding to feelings at the verbal or "symbolic" behavior level, an officer can keep the person's words from turning to action. Also, responding to feelings at a verbal level can give an officer the necessary clues to determine the citizen's intention. If they become quiet after an officer has responded to their feelings, they may be telling the officer that they are going to act on them; on the other hand, if they go with it verbally, they are telling the officer that they want to talk it out instead of acting on it. It is obvious what the difference is between a talking fight where the parties are looking for a way out ("Yeah" versus

"Oh, yeah!") and a real fight where the fists will be flying at any second.

Besides being able to defuse negative feelings so that words don't become negative actions, responding to feelings leads to greater understanding of a citizen. A citizen cannot always link up their feelings with the situation and is often at a loss to understand what they are thinking. In addition, when an officer responds to positive feelings, these feelings get reinforced (unlike negative feelings). There is nothing mysterious about this. No one enjoys negative feelings, so people get rid of them by sharing them—by "talking it out." But people do enjoy positive feelings. They only become stronger when they are shared with another person. Officers can choose to strengthen the positive feelings that will help a citizen act more positively simply by recognizing and responding to those feelings. As a general rule, a person who feels positively about him- or herself will try to do positive things, while a person who feels negatively about him- or herself will try to do negative things. If you push this out, you arrive at the general principle: *"People tend to act in ways consistent with the way other significant people see and act toward them."*

To effectively respond to feeling, officers need to position and posture their bodies, then observe and listen. Then, officers need to reflect for the feeling (happy, angry, sad, scared) and its intensity (high, medium, or low). Finally, an officer may respond by saying:

> "You feel <insert word here>." For example, "You feel <u>angry</u>."

Here, the new skill involves reflecting for feeling and intensity. Adding a new skill doesn't mean discarding the old skills, of course. When reflecting for feeling, officers are really asking themselves, "Given what I see and hear, how does this citizen basically feel?" Are they happy, angry, sad, scared, or confused? This citizen's behavior and words will give an officer a good indication of the feeling. For example, a person who shouts at another person, "You stupid idiot, now look what you've done!" while they shake their fist and get red in the face is obviously feeling a level of anger.

After the feeling word has been selected, the officer must reflect on the intensity of the feeling. For example, anger can be high in intensity (boiling mad), medium in intensity (frustrated), or low in intensity (concern). The more accurately the feeling word reflects the intensity, the more effective a response will be. That is, an officer's response will be more accurate and will do the job better (e.g., defuse the negative feeling). One wouldn't choose "concerned" for the above example because the term is too weak to describe a man yelling, shaking his fist, and turning red. Such an embarrassment would probably only make them angrier. But, "You feel furious" would fit fine.

Making the Point: Responding to Feeling

Deputy John Sheridan is a sheriff's deputy for a local Sheriff's Office. He is assigned to the bureau of the Sheriff's Office responsible for serving civil papers and subpoenas. Deputy Sheridan has worked in this assignment for many years and observed many different reactions from people displaying anger, sadness, confusion, or hysteria. Deputy Sheridan never knows what the reaction will be from people once they understand why he is present and they comprehend what message he has been sent to deliver.

One morning, Deputy Sheridan served a civil court action to Steve Harris. Harris was at work and his supervisor asked him to step into the front office. Upon entering the office,

Harris' supervisor stepped out while introducing Harris to Deputy Sheridan, who was waiting for Harris to arrive. Deputy Sheridan explained to Harris that he needed to provide court documents to him regarding divorce proceedings that his wife of 25 years had initiated.

Harris displayed a multitude of emotions upon hearing the news from Deputy Sheridan. Harris began to cry and shake his head from side to side while stating, "I just don't understand why she is doing this. I have been a great husband and father. She told me that she didn't love me anymore. How did this happen? I didn't think she would take it this far."

Deputy Sheridan responded by stating, "Steve, I understand that you feel very confused and that you feel like you've done everything possible to save your marriage. Is there someone I can call to assist you while you adjust to learning this news today?"

In this scenario, Deputy Sheridan not only completed his official job duty of serving the civil paper to Steve Harris, but he also observed and listened to Steve and offered support by showing respect and dignity. This small gesture lets Steve Harris know that Deputy Sheridan was empathetic, respectful, and allowed him voice during the encounter.

THE THIRD PART OF RESPONDING

Responding to feeling and meaning. Responding to feeling and meaning combines the two previous skills. Responding to feeling and meaning requires you to paraphrase the content of another person's statement in such a way as to provide a meaningful reason for the person's feeling.

The two steps in responding to feeling and meaning are: 1) reflect on the feeling and the reason for that feeling, and 2) respond to the feeling and meaning.

Learning how to respond to content and how to respond to feeling has prepared you to respond to feeling and meaning. Now your response at this new level can put everything together. Here you will capture effectively where the person is at the moment. By adding meaning to the feeling, you will help yourself and the other person understand the reason for their feelings about the situation. The reason is simply the personal meaning for the other person about what is happening. For example, an officer in danger of being pulled into a fight when their record is clean and their promotion coming up might feel "afraid" because "the fight could blow my chances to get promoted." Moreover, the officer might be fearful of media exposure if he or she were to use force to affect an arrest. The personal meaning of the potential fight for this officer is that it might blow their chances of promotion. That is one reason why they hesitated, not that they are scared of fighting, but of not getting the promotion. Another reason might be that they were fearful of disciplinary action or wide-scale media attention for using force.

By combining the feeling and meaning and responding to both, an officer will show the other person that they understand their experience as they present it. This increases the chances of the person talking about the thing in which the officer is interested. In addition, for supervision purposes, an officer will be able to learn more about what the supervisee values and what bothers them so they can get a handle on them and, if necessary, use the values and knowledge to apply pressure on them. For example, a supervisor might be confronted with an officer who is refusing to take responsibility for losing their temper.

Making the Point: Responding to Feeling and Meaning

> In another situation, a citizen discusses a concern he has about his teenage son:
>
> **Citizen:** "He's headed for trouble. I just can't control him anymore. All he listens to are the punks he runs with."
>
> **Officer:** "You feel worried because you know that unless your son wakes up, he's going to be just like them."
>
> **Citizen:** "Yeah. They are into drugs and none of them work. You know what's going to happen when you see that."
>
> **Officer:** "You feel kind of scared because you can see how the drug problem leads to other problems for kids."
>
> **Citizen:** "Right, and it's getting worse all the time and I don't know what to do."
>
> **Officer:** "Is he in school?"
>
> **Citizen:** "Yeah, he goes to the vo-tech school downtown."

The officer understands clearly where the citizen is in the situation, where he wants (or needs) to be, and is able to suggest a possible solution. This became possible because the officer was able to attach an understanding of meaning to the feelings of the citizen.

By building on what has been learned, an officer adds the reason to the feeling response they have just learned. The new way of responding becomes "You feel _____ because _____."

What needs to be the focus here, of course, is an individual's reason (personal meaning) for their feeling. Supplying the reason means that one must understand why what has happened is important. This is accomplished by rephrasing the content in one's own words to capture that importance. Officers are actually giving the reason for the feeling. In this way, they make the person's feeling clearer and more understandable.

It is also important to capture whether a person is seeing him- or herself as responsible or seeing someone else as responsible. An officer's response should reflect where he or she sees the responsibility in the beginning, even though they might not agree. By doing this, you will have a better chance of opening them up. You can always disagree when it becomes necessary and effective to do so. Remember, if you have this skill, you can choose to use it. If not, no choice.

The following scenario reflects an example of a way that a law enforcement supervisor could respond to an officer who approaches them with a problem. The officer is frustrated and says to the supervisor: "You know this job takes its toll on police marriages and nobody in this organization cares."

What does this situation really mean to the officer? Who is the officer blaming? Why is all of this so important to them? What does this mean to him or her? A supervisor should put him- or herself in the other person's place. Once the meaning is recognized, there is need to formulate a response.

The supervisor who was actually involved knew how to initiate communication with this officer in a tense situation like this—and they recognized that failure to do so could mean trouble. The supervisor knew that the officer's basic feeling was *upset*, the intensity of this feeling was *high*, and that the officer was really *furious*. And the supervisor knew that the officer was blaming the *demands of the organization* for his marital problems, whether true or not, which was the meaning of the situation for the officer.

Knowing all of this, the supervisor was able to respond effectively to the feeling and to what this feeling meant: "You feel upset because you believe that this organization doesn't care how it affects an officer's marriage." This response surprised the officer. He had expected the supervisor to deny everything; to tell them to grow up; to ignore the whole thing or to simply state "that's just how it is— they forget what it's like on the front line." He certainly did not expect the supervisor to respond to their situation at the same level that they were experiencing it.

Because the supervisor knew how to respond at this level, they were able to keep the officer talking openly. And in a tense situation, this can mean the difference between an effective supervisor and an ineffective supervisor.

When responding to feeling and meaning, a communication interchange may sometimes go deeper than one might be able to handle. If this happens, an officer must consider the option of a referral (to an employee assistance program, perhaps.) With the supervisor's added understanding, the referral will be that much more specific and beneficial.

But many times, an officer's added understanding will provide the information needed to really understand people. The payoff will be rewarding. Many officers put in their time but don't get the payoff because they lack some of the skills needed to finish the good start that they made by being decent and fair. Responding is one way to ensure that payoff.

Asking Questions

Officers ask questions in order to get useful answers. Some questions get better answers than others: the skill of asking questions will help increase the information base and thus an officer's ability to manage others.

Two Steps in Asking Questions

As the following materials make clear, there are really two basic steps involved in asking relevant questions in an effective way:

1. Using the 5WH method

2. Reflecting on answers and recycling

Having responded to a person at the most accurate level, an officer must first develop one or more questions of the 5WH type: who, what, where, when, why, and how. Second, reflect upon the answer or answers given by the person to make sure you fully understand all of the implications. Did you get the information you wanted? Was new information revealed?

Asking questions will help you effectively communicate. If a person answered your questions satisfactorily, officers would be all set. After all, officers have all the right questions. The reality, however, is that for a variety of reasons (e.g., lack of trust, guilt) many people do not answer questions fully or accurately. In fact, questions will sometimes have the opposite effect: the person will shut off communication with people rather than open up. This is because questions are often seen as the bullets of the enemy ("Cover up, here they come"). The only way questions can be really effective in opening up a person is when they are used in addition to the basic skills plus responding. Use of the basics plus responding can get a person to the point where they will talk openly. It is then that questions can make their contribution by getting some of the necessary specifics (who, what, when, where, why and how—the 5WH system).

THE FIRST PART IN ASKING QUESTIONS

Asking 5WH questions. Answers to questions will give officers the details needed to communicate with people effectively. The more details you know, the better you can understand what is going on. Officers always want to know who is involved, what they are doing or going to do, when and where something happened or will happen, how it was done or is going to be done, and why it did or will take place:

> "Where were you?"
> "Who were you with?"
> "Why were you there?"
> "What did you actually do?"
> "When did all this happen?"
> "How was it handled?"

When officers have all of this information, they can take appropriate action and/or prevent problems from happening (now and maybe in the future). Question-asking can be used with responding during an interrogation, interview, or when the officer chooses to assist with a problem.

Responding gets the person to open up, providing the opportunity to make sure you understand what is being said. It also builds trust. For these reasons, always try to respond to the other person's actions or words at the highest possible level before actually starting to ask questions. Questions then fill in the details of the picture. Often, details (reasons) come from responding skills alone if officers have patience. If they do not, questions are appropriate.

THE SECOND PART IN ASKING QUESTIONS

Reflecting on answers to questions. It is not enough just to ask good questions. Law enforcement officers also have to be able to make sense out of the answers (and recognize, as well perhaps, the answers that are still not being received).

Begin by responding to the answer:

"You're saying _____ " or "So you feel _____."

Then reflect on or think carefully about the answer to your question.

The person might be leveling with the officer asking the question and giving the information needed to understand things or provide assistance. They might be leveling with the officer as best they can but perhaps not giving all the information needed. Or they might be covering something up, which means that they are still not opening up fully, still not really communicating with the officer asking questions. An officer's observation skills are critical here.

In reflecting on the person's answer to the question, an officer can consider four specific things:

1. How does the person look as they answer (relaxed, uncomfortable)

2. What is the person doing while they answer (facing you and making eye contact, looking away, looking down at their feet)

3. What has the person actually said (the information content of the answer)

4. What might they have failed to say (any "gaps" in the way their answer fits with your questions).

By reflecting on these four areas of concern, an officer can make sure that they fully understand all the implications of the answer. Once the officer has responded to this answer, they can ask additional questions to get the rest of the information needed. By using the basics—responding, asking good questions, reflecting, and then responding again, etc., the officer is effectively recycling.

Making the Point: Reflecting on Answers

Officer Christopher Reed was dispatched to a report of a fight in progress at the intersection of Main Street and Elm Street. While driving to the incident location, Officer Reed was advised via police radio that a traffic accident occurred just minutes prior and now four males were physically fighting in the roadway, causing an obstruction to the normal traffic flow.

Officer Reed arrived on location and observed two vehicles in the roadway with damage, and other vehicles driving around the scene. Officer Reed didn't observe any males fighting, but was met by a hysterical adult female who screamed multiple things at Officer Reed as he exited his patrol vehicle. The female was very excited and upset and told Officer Reed, "Oh my gosh, that guy hit us and then tried to leave…I think he's drunk…my boyfriend tried to keep him here, but he ran into the woods."

Officer Reed asked the female for her name, her boyfriend's name, and which vehicle she was traveling in at the time of the accident. He also asked for a physical description of her boyfriend, the other driver, and any other people involved who ran into the wooded area. The female stated that only her boyfriend and the other driver were involved, and no other people. This question answers **"Who"** and confirmed that there is now conflicting information as to what the dispatcher was told by a passing motorist (four males were fighting) and what the female involved witnessed (two males—her boyfriend and the other driver).

Officer Reed advised responding units of the physical description of the two males and their direction of travel. He then used "The Basics" and attempted to determine what happened during the incident. This is a very fluid scene with many things taking place, so "The Basics" obviously need to be used with officer safety as the highest priority. Officer Reed determined what transpired, when the incident happened, confirmed where the incident started and ended, and did the best he could in determining how the incident began and ended. During the entire process, Officer Reed arranged himself appropriately, and positioned and postured himself to be most effective. Officer Reed also observed and listened to what was being communicated to him in order to ask quality **Questions** related to the incident.

Summary of the Add-ons

Jimmy was an inmate who everyone—officers and other inmates alike—invariably referred to as "a bad dude." There was a lot of respect in this phrase. You learned respect around Jimmy. How could you help it? He was 6 feet 5 inches, 275 pounds, and a former sergeant in the Green Berets. To top it off, he had a temper like a bear just coming out of hibernation who found the ground was still frozen solid.

Jimmy didn't like officers. In his time, he'd sent more than a few to the hospital. By now, the officers had figured out a drill. When they wanted Jimmy out of his cell, six of them went in and brought him out. Even then it wasn't easy.

One day a lieutenant who had been on the street came on to begin his duty as the police department detention administrator. The old hands were happy to show him around. "Listen," they said. "You need to meet Jimmy."

"Jimmy?" The lieutenant didn't have a whole lot of experience in handling people in the department lockup, but he knew a set-up when he saw one. Half a dozen seasoned officers accompanied the lieutenant to Jimmy's cell, grinning and nudging each other. Oh, they wouldn't let the lieutenant get hurt or anything, they just wanted to know if the lieutenant had been sitting in the office too long.

"Hey, Jimmy—you got someone to see you," one of the officers told the huge inmate, unlocking the cell and moving back quickly. "You said you wanted to talk to the new director of the lockup".

Jimmy's only answer was a grunt. He had been sleeping. Now he emerged slowly from his bunk scowling and rubbing his eyes.

"What do you miserable creeps want now? Man, I'm going to tear somebody into small pieces if you come close enough!" His eyes focused on the lieutenant for the first time. "What's this, some kind of bait or something?"

The older officers expected the lieutenant to back off when he saw Jimmy towering over him. Instead, the new man stuck out his hand.

"I'm Lieutenant Ben Jones," he said. "I guess you're really upset at us for just barging in on you."

The other officers saw Jimmy's brow furrow. He'd been about to swing and they'd been all tensed up to jump in. But now Jimmy seemed unsure. He didn't shake. But he also didn't swing.

Then his face cleared. In another moment, he flung his head back and laughed out loud. "Whooeee!" He calmed down at last and looked at the lieutenant. "I knew it! I knew if I just hung around this place long enough they'd have to send in a real human being to handle me!"

And that was it. In choosing to initiate communication instead of using force, the lieutenant had taken Jimmy off guard. This was a new approach. More than that, it was an indication to an inmate full of anger and hostility that maybe there still were people out there who could talk to him—even listen to him. And that knowledge made all the difference in the world to Jimmy!

What enabled the lieutenant to make this kind of difference, of course, was his communication skills—in particular, **Responding.** And these are the same skills you yourself have begun to master.

It is important to note that officers must determine if there is "trouble" or "no trouble" when deciding to use social tactics. Sometimes, situations and actions of others happen so quickly that the use of social tactics would be virtually impossible due to the threat that has presented itself. This chapter explained ways that officers could use social tactics when they have decided that the situation is appropriate to do so. By asking relevant questions and responding with interest and concern, citizens are more likely to open up and talk more freely with law enforcement officers.

Officers must frequently ask themselves, "Is the decision that I am about to make objectively reasonable and what any other officer with my level of tenure, experience, and training do?" When the situation is appropriate, it is important for officers to attempt to build a rapport with an individual to create trust and show respect. This will ulti-mately lead to a better interaction.

Chapter 5

Safety–Assess–Decide–ACTION

Two of the most frequent tasks that law enforcement officers perform on a daily basis is handling requests from other people and making requests of other people. Citizens, business owners, and visitors to a particular jurisdiction almost never ask law enforcement officers to respond to a location because of something happy or positive. Almost always, law enforcement officers are requested to respond to and handle a request from a person who needs law enforcement action. The circumstances may relate to a domestic dispute, theft from a vehicle, a business owner who wants to report a shoplifting incident, or a civil matter or a traffic accident. The list is endless regarding the numerous types of calls for service that law enforcement officers receive, but one thing is true: the general public wants law enforcement officers to handle frequent requests on a daily basis. Officers handle dozens of requests during each shift from a very diverse community consisting of differing ethnicities, personalities, and social backgrounds. Yet, officers are required to respond and meet with victims, witnesses, and suspects, and interact effectively with all of these different types of people while determining how to properly act and handle their requests.

Not only do law enforcement officers handle dozens of requests each work day, they also make requests many times during each shift. Officers make requests of fellow officers and supervisors while also making requests of the people they encounter in the field during their shift. When officers make requests of other people, the way that the request is made (tone, volume, choice of wording) will often determine the outcome and how the receiver chooses to comply with the request. Sometimes, officers make requests of people who are under the influence of drugs or alcohol. Additionally, other factors might affect how the request is made by the officer, such as the mental status or a potential disability of the person.

There are many instances in which law enforcement officers encounter where they have absolutely no time to attempt verbal communication because the person is violent to the point that the officer must intervene using physical tactics. An example of this would be an officer arriving to the scene of a domestic dispute and upon walking up to the house, the officer observes through the front window that a male is holding down a female and using an object to strike her numerous times in the head. This would be a good example of how the officer would immediately use some form of force (non-deadly force or deadly force), depending on the circumstances, to stop the threat.

The social tactic skills associated with action combine the basic skills and the skills of how to decide. All of these skills are aimed at controlling behavior. These skills are important in helping an officer maintain control and communicate well with other people.

The action skills used in controlling behavior are:

1. Handling requests
2. Making requests
3. Reinforcing behavior

Making the Point: Controlling Behavior

Lieutenant Jim Smith has a reputation for applying the rules when they suit him and always saying "No" just because he feels like it.

Jim has been married to his wife for 18 years. Both of their children moved out of the house following high school. Jim's wife informed him that she wanted a divorce, now that the children are gone. She told Jim their marriage for the most part was a failure due to Jim's over-controlling nature and his "know it all attitude" toward her and the children.

Jim was shocked because he knew they had problems, but not to the degree to cause a divorce.

One evening, Jim was drinking at his favorite bar. He was feeling very depressed because his wife had just moved out of their house, leaving him alone. Jim, knowing that he had too much to drink, called three fellow officers for a ride home. All three of them said they were busy and suggested he take a cab.

Jim became angry after the third officer told him no. The officer told him that he was off duty and there was no obligation to pick him up. Jim decided to drive his vehicle home despite having had a few drinks.

Approximately five minutes from home, he was stopped by a state trooper. Jim got out of his car and identified himself as a police lieutenant. Jim was expecting "officer courtesy" from a fellow officer.

The trooper wanted to see Jim's driver's license. Jim refused, stating who he was. The trooper was young and "by the book." He told Jim he didn't care who he was. Jim became irate and a scuffle ensued between Jim and the trooper.

Eventually, backup troopers arrived and Jim was arrested for DUI and a misdemeanor obstruction of a law enforcement officer. He was booked into the county jail.

The moral of this story is not that Jim should have been given officer courtesy, but that Jim's style of managing people had been arbitrary his whole life. Yet when Jim experienced someone like himself, he became angry and combative. If Jim had developed effective social intelligence skills earlier in his career, he might have prevented the above. He might have preserved his marriage and family. He might also have ensured that any fellow officer would have done whatever he needed when he needed them, whether on or off duty. Jim's poor controlling skills, of himself as well as others, led to his demise.

Controlling behavior simply means taking charge. This is what it is all about in law enforcement. Without the ability to control behavior, all the other efforts are wasted. An officer has to do everything he or she can to ensure appropriate behavior; in the interests of society, in themselves, and in the interest of supervisees. The same holds true for all people. Learning to control our behavior is in the best interest of everyone. Without control, nothing productive can or will occur.

This chapter builds on previous chapters. It is about the "how" of controlling behavior by using good communication skills.

The Three Application Skills

As mentioned earlier, the skills used in controlling behavior are handling requests, making requests, and reinforcing behavior.

Unlike the skills in previous chapters, these three areas are not all cumulative. That is, a person will be involved at any given time in either handling requests or making requests. In either situation, however, an officer will want to reinforce the behavior—positively if the desire is for someone to keep doing a particular thing, and negatively if the desire is to keep him from doing something.

Before going any further, the following example is provided to show these skills in action. The situation described below is quite routine and details where a supervisor demonstrates skill in management. It could be handled much differently with more negative outcomes. It involves both the law enforcement supervisee making a request and, in turn, a request being handled by their supervisor.

Making the Point: Handling Requests

Sergeant Joan Wilson:	"Larry, I'd like you to switch your shift with Roderick for the next two weeks because he has been having problems and needs to be off on the weekends for personal reasons."
Officer Larry Wright:	"Is it okay with you if I try to get someone else to do it? I'd like to keep my schedule as it is because I started bowling in a league."
Sergeant Joan Wilson:	"I'm sorry, Larry. I know that would upset your schedule, but I can't use anyone else since you are the only one who can switch in your unit. I've already checked it out with the other guys. It will only be for two weeks."
Officer Larry Wright:	"Why do you always pick on me? I'm always the one who gets screwed on these deals?"
Sergeant Joan Wilson:	"I know this irritates you greatly because it will interrupt your routine, but it's the best I can do right now. Please assume this new schedule one week from today's date and then you'll rotate back to your normal schedule after the two-week period is complete."

Although the above situation involves communications between a supervisor and a supervisee, the same principle could be applied to an officer-citizen encounter. All law enforcement officers can think of many examples where an officer asks a citizen to do something that the citizen may not want to do. However, in the above example, the sergeant used her skills to control this situation. She didn't demean or put down, she didn't use sarcasm. You will observe, however, that included in her skills were firmness and reasons for her actions. There was no weakness. The officer now knows what he is expected to do and why. The sergeant was even able to continue to be responsive to the officer when the officer became irritated. The use of skill gets the job done and increases the probability that the officer will feel he has been treated fairly, even if he has to have his routine interrupted—quite by contrast when one thinks about how it might have been handled.

The above example also shows how important it is to practice a procedural justice mindset. By Officer Wright feeling that he has been treated fairly by his supervisor in this situation, he might be more inclined to treat others fairly and ultimately be successful in controlling the behavior of others on calls for service.

Handling Requests

Handling requests is the ability to manage requests in a fair and effective manner. The skillful handling of requests helps build trust and reduce tension.

The two steps in handling requests are: Check things out and give a response or reason. Handling requests is action. Law enforcement officers frequently "check things out" during a shift and also "give responses" to others. How the individual officer chooses to handle or respond to a request could ultimately determine if the incident ends calmly and peacefully or if a person or group of people become irate based on how the officer chose to handle the request.

THE FIRST PART OF HANDLING REQUESTS

Checking out the person and situation. It goes without saying that officers are and will be receiving requests from people. Some will be legitimate, some not. Each request must be, and is, responded to. Even if an officer ignores the request, they have responded to it and some consequence will occur that can affect their ability to handle and control people. If officers find this hard to believe, they should put themselves in a situation where they want their shift supervisor to consider one of their own requests which gets ignored.

Before officers respond to any request, they need to use their basic skills to check out the person who makes it. Are they trustworthy or are they trying to pull one over on you? Officers also need to check out the situation in terms of any policies or regulations that might apply. Using positioning, observing, listening, and responding skills will be invaluable in this situation.

By knowing which of the communicating skills to use, one can ensure that they know what is happening with a particular person who has a request. By reviewing the appropriate rules and regulations, one will be able to determine if the request is or is not legitimate.

THE SECOND PART OF HANDLING REQUESTS

Responding with a reason for the decision. The new skill here involves indicating the action the officer is going to take—the decision—and giving the person a reason. **Giving the other person a good reason is not a sign of weakness.**

On the contrary, it is the best way in which to minimize future complaints. If officers have to tell a citizen something they will not like, they won't be able to complain that you didn't even tell them why. And if an officer grants their request, they'll know that it was just for this one situation for a good and clear reason.

Basically, an officer has three possible avenues of action in relation to a request. In each case, they should give some reason for their action. Here are some formats that can be used:

Responding with Reason for Decisions

- "Yes, I'll do (it) _____ because _____."
- "No, I won't do (it) _____ because _____."
- "I'll look into (it) _____ because _____."

In each instance, the officer bases their intent on the laws and regulations that apply. In cases where people need or request something beyond what they are entitled to by law and regulation, each person's behavior (past and present), what is asked for, the way it is asked for, and the information officers have gained by checking things out, may determine their response. For example, a supervisor was called by a supervisee's spouse that asked, "Can you talk to my husband about our marital problems? He says he's working overtime and that's why he's not coming home." You, as the supervisor, know that the officer hasn't been working overtime.

While a supervisor may have an option in a case like the above, some things—like responding to a supervisee in distress—cannot be denied. Officers may have options for an abusive citizen who demands attention, but they cannot deny the emergency service that is warranted. Knowing the law and the regulations of the agency will definitely make an officer's job easier—especially with all the grievances that are initiated these days. Yet by taking care of the basic rights or needs of citizens and co-workers, tensions will be greatly reduced.

Taking care of basic rights or needs is a must in any relationship. It would be very hard for a citizen or co-worker to believe an officer wanted to assist them if they did not attend to their basic rights or needs—that is, if an officer did not give them what they were entitled to (sometimes beyond policy or roles.) Dealing with such rights or needs in a concrete way builds trust that will make it more likely that people will get the trust and support they and an agency wants from the employees and citizens.

Making the Point: Responding with a Reason for a Decision

Officer Morris is assigned to the Special Operations Division and his primary duty is to enforce the traffic laws of the state. One evening, he stopped a traffic violator for speeding over 15 miles per hour above the posted speed limit.

Officer Morris made contact with the driver and introduced himself while also stating the reason for the traffic stop. After obtaining the driver's license, the driver asked Officer Morris if it would be possible to receive a warning for the violation. Officer Morris asked the driver why he was asking for a warning.

The driver responded that he had never received a citation and has been driving for almost 20 years. The driver added that his wife just called him while he was at work and told him that her doctor just informed her that she had stage 4 breast cancer. The driver added that he was very upset upon receiving this information and was trying to get to the doctor's office to be with his wife, as she was hysterical. The driver was very apologetic and stated that he would obey the speed limit in the future and thanked Officer Morris for pointing out the infraction.

Officer Morris responded, "Yes, I will not issue a citation and only provide you with a verbal warning because of your unique circumstances and driving history." Officer Morris wished the driver well as he started to leave and the driver responded, "Thank you for showing kindness in my time of need. God bless you, officer."

In this scenario, Officer Morris not only used "The Basics" but also observed, listened, responded, and above all else, displayed dignity and respect after giving voice during this encounter.

Making Requests

Making requests is the ability to communicate with people by making specific requests of them. Making requests skillfully improves the chances that people will cooperate and more readily carry out your requests.

The two procedures involved in making requests in an effective way are:

1. Checking things out (using the same procedures as when an officer is handling requests)

2. Taking appropriate action

Officers need to check things out to ensure that they do not make the wrong move—a move that might increase tension rather than calm things down. Once this has been accomplished, the officer can decide whether the best action will involve a simple request, an order, or even direct physical action.

THE FIRST PART OF MAKING REQUESTS

Checking things out. Since the procedures here will be the same as those involved in handling requests, there is no need to go back over them at length. Here, however, the aim should be to understand as much as possible about the situation involving the person who an officer plans to have do something. Are they with family members or friends? Are they someone with a prior history of having problems? Will they feel embarrassed if they are told to do something and therefore react antagonistically? Are they in the midst of doing something already and officer or supervisor intervention will be interrupting them? By using basic sizing up and responding skills, if there is any tension in the air, one can make sure that whatever action is taken in making the request will be effective.

THE SECOND PART OF MAKING REQUESTS

Taking appropriate action. Making requests of other people is routine when supervising or policing people, of course. Many requests are made each shift and often, little thought is given to the impact of those requests both on the control of co-workers or citizens and their immediate and long-term cooperation. It is how the request is made that often makes the difference, not the nature of the request.

In taking action to get a citizen or a co-worker to do something, remember that officers have to be specific. Officers need to always remember to effectively communicate. An officer should identify what should be done and when. Many officers and most of their supervisors have learned that a polite request is effective in getting citizens to do what they are being asked to do.

Of course, there are officers who feel that uncooperative citizens or citizens who are frequent problems don't deserve politeness or that being polite makes an officer look weak. Keeping in mind the procedural justice mindset, officers need to always treat others with dignity and respect. Is it appropriate to allow the uncooperative citizen to bring the officer down to their level? In addition, when a citizen doesn't do something reasonable when asked politely, then it is they who look weak and not the officer. Moreover, by being initially polite, the officer has given the citizen the opportunity to go the easy route. Now it is their responsibility if the officer has to react with a stronger approach.

Some officers are going to find it difficult to use a polite format, but many officers have found that it is more effective to be polite. It gets the desired results. A mild (polite) request can take the form "Would you (please) _____ " or it can take the form "I would appreciate it if you would _____ ."

When you make a request, the most direct method is simply to identify what you desire and then use the format "I want you to _____ ." But because people often resent authority if you are simply telling them to do something, you might have fewer hassles if you use more of a polite or mild request format. Examples might be "I'd like you to do _____ " or "Would you stop _____ ."

An officer can soften the statement even more by using polite words. For example, "I'd like you to please stop _____ ." What format an officer uses for making a request will depend on the situation and the particular citizen. Of course, if a person abuses the mild method, officers are always free to move to a stronger position, including a more direct but lawful order. As indicated above, the point is to get the job done—to have the person do what an officer needs them to do. Most experienced officers agree that in the long term, it is generally better if direct confrontation can be avoided. An officer may also want to use responding skills in taking action.

Making the Point: Taking Appropriate Action

Deputy Mario Aguilar graduated from the law enforcement academy nine years ago and began working for a Sheriff's Office. He has been assigned to uniform patrol duties since he began his career and is considered a deputy who is proactive. Although Deputy Aguilar is proactive, he occasionally will have citizens call to complain about his attitude and demeanor. Citizens will occasionally report that Deputy Aguilar was rude or disrespectful while he interacted with them. Over the past nine years, Deputy Aguilar established a certain way of handling tasks which include how he chooses to interact with citizens in the performance of his duties.

Prior to attending the class. Deputy Aguilar would initiate a traffic stop, approach the driver, and simply state "Driver's license and insurance card." Additionally, Deputy Aguilar would ask the driver, "Do you know why you were stopped?" Depending on what the driver's response was to this question, Deputy Aguilar would ensure that the driver knew the reason for the stop and walk back to his vehicle, never allowing the driver to have voice or explain any circumstance that may be the reason for the driver committing the traffic violation.

After attending training on ways to more effectively communicate, Deputy Aguilar decided to practice the techniques he learned in training when performing future traffic stops. He decided that he was "going to give this stuff a shot" to see if it really works. Deputy Aguilar understands that all traffic stops are far from routine and that different circumstances exist with every stop. Knowing and understanding this, Deputy Aguilar initiated a traffic stop, intending to use the newly-learned techniques.

Deputy Aguilar initiated the traffic stop on a red passenger car for a stop sign violation. He decided to change his normal approach when first making contact with the driver. As he tactically approached the vehicle, he made contact with the driver, stating, "Good afternoon, I am Deputy Aguilar with the Gray County Sheriff's Office. May I see your driver's license and insurance card?" The driver responded, "Sure." While the driver is retrieving the requested items, Deputy Aguilar tells the driver, "Sir, the reason for the traffic stop today is because I observed your vehicle not come to a complete stop at the intersection of Lakeview Drive and Piedmont Street. Is there a reason that your vehicle didn't come to a complete stop?"

The driver responded that he felt that slowing down enough to view if any oncoming traffic was approaching was sufficient. The driver also explained that he was late to an appointment and asked Deputy Aguilar to not issue a citation. Deputy Aguilar advised the driver that the law states that drivers must come to a complete stop and to ensure that there is no oncoming traffic prior to proceeding into the intersection. The driver stated that he understood and apologized.

Deputy Aguilar returned to his patrol vehicle, checked the driver's license and license plate to ensure that there were no issues, and then returned to the vehicle. He told the driver that no citation will be issued in this incident, but future violations would result in a citation being issued. The driver stated that he understood and apologized again while telling Deputy Aguilar, "Thank you for all you do. I am the President of the Chamber of Commerce and it is good to know that we have deputies like you representing our community."

The intent in traffic stops is not to ruin a citizen's day or to harass them. The intent is to modify behavior and to make the streets safer for motorists. In the above instance, Deputy Aguilar accomplished the goal of enforcing traffic laws, which is a requirement of his job, but he also did much more. By beginning the interaction in a positive manner, he set the tone for the entire traffic stop. A lot of times, law enforcement officers forget what it is like to be on the other side of the traffic stop. It is a very tense and sometimes nerve-racking experience for a driver. Deputy Aguilar's polite and courteous tone from the very beginning presented a positive image of himself and his agency. He made the initial request for the driver's license and insurance card knowing his lawful authority, but in this case *asking* to view the items rather than simply stating, "Driver's license and insurance card." Of course, Deputy Aguilar knew that state law required the driver to provide the driver's license upon lawful request of a law enforcement officer during a traffic stop. However, he chose the politeness route during this instance and it paid off. Deputy Aguilar learned that one never knows who is in the driver's seat of a vehicle when a traffic stop is initiated. By showing respect for the driver initially and giving voice during the encounter, Deputy Aguilar learned that there could potentially be better outcomes to situations.

Of course, not every incident has a citizen responding in a positive manner to politeness displayed by the law enforcement officer. Sometimes, citizens will not respond in a positive manner but will be very rude, disrespectful, and in some cases disorderly no matter how polite the law enforcement officer is to them during the encounter. In cases such as this, law enforcement officers should know that when internal affairs investigators and juries view or listen to the incident via audio/video, it helps the officer to present the image of being polite and courteous from the very beginning of the encounter. Most IA investigators and persons on a jury will think to themselves that the deputy or officer was very nice and polite from the very beginning of the incident and the citizen is the one who was rude and disrespectful from the beginning.

Reinforcing Behavior

Reinforcing behavior means attaching or withdrawing something pleasant associated with a behavior. Punishment means associating unpleasant consequences with a behavior. Reinforcing and non-reinforcing behaviors may either be verbal or nonverbal.

The four steps of reinforcing/non-reinforcing behavior are reinforcing verbally, reinforcing nonverbally, non-reinforcing verbally, and non-reinforcing nonverbally.

The only reason people finally do anything is because of the consequences (positive or negative) of doing it or not doing it. Behaviors only change when there are consequences. There are clearly examples of people being rewarded for inappropriate (bad) behavior. Criminals who go uncaught are reinforced by the attention and material gain. Whining children are given sweets to quiet them in grocery stores. Police officers may receive the adulation of their peers for their expression of force. This often reinforces negative behavior to continue which is not appropriate.

Using rewards and punishment appropriately can have both short-term and long-term positive potential when interacting with others. It can enhance the likelihood of responsible behavior from citizens immediately and also assist in more long-term outcomes such as citizen cooperation and support.

As an officer, one can be a *"reinforcer"* by giving verbal and/or nonverbal responses as ways to maintain and/or increased desired behaviors.

Verbal reinforcement means expressing orally something an officer knows is pleasantly experienced by a person and associating it with some positive, responsible behavior: "Sir, thank you for removing your vehicle from the roadway after the collision took place. By doing this, you allowed traffic to begin flowing normally which relieved the congestion." or "Sir, I appreciated you taking responsibility for running the red light—most people that I stop want to deny committing the offense."

Reinforcing nonverbally means adding the reinforcement without using words. The most obvious would be smiling, nodding the head, etc. A person who moves their vehicle to provide a larger space for better pedestrian movement and gets a nod and a smile is an example of giving nonverbal reinforcement.

Some nonverbal cues might be intended to reinforce a behavior, but actually might be experienced as less than pleasant. For example, Officer Johnson is having difficulty using the new accident reporting software to complete a traffic accident report and asks Sergeant Robinson for assistance. Sergeant Robinson walks over to Officer Johnson, showing a willingness to assist with the problem. As soon as Sergeant Robinson views the computer screen, he immediately can see what Officer Johnson is doing wrong. As Officer Johnson uses the computer mouse, he is about to select an option that will delete his entire report. Sergeant Robinson grabs Officer Johnson's hand and jerks it away from the mouse, giving him a critical facial expression that implies he is stupid. Then he shows Officer Johnson the correct way to complete the report. Sergeant Robinson's intent may have been to reinforce his willingness to help and educate Officer Johnson regarding the correct way to complete the report, but the way he conducted himself may have left Officer Johnson with an unpleasant feeling.

Verbal non-reinforcing means saying something with the intention of decreasing or eliminating an undesirable behavior. These can be some of the most difficult conversations;

therefore, one's ability to size up a situation and use the skills previously discussed in this book will be invaluable. Being polite can be an officer's best approach. Examples of verbal non-reinforcement can be mild, such as, "Please do not interrupt while the other driver is telling me their side of what occurred in the traffic accident" or an intense "Stop it NOW!"

Insults and hurtful statements are also examples of verbal non-reinforcement. An example would be an officer who tells a traffic violator, "I can't believe that you blocked that intersection. You must be illiterate not to have read the four signs posted at the intersection telling motorists not to block the intersection!"

Nonverbal reinforcing means using nonverbal cues to decrease or eliminate undesired behaviors. The most obvious nonverbal cues are the shaking of one's head back and forth indicating "No" or "Stop," looking a citizen with a serious expression that communicates displeasure, and rolling of the eyes. Other nonverbal reinforcing involves withholding behaviors that one might normally do to another person in an effort to reduce or eliminate an undesired behavior. For example, after being criticized by a supervisor for focusing too much time on traffic enforcement, an officer may decide to not do any traffic stops for a while and be non-productive during slow times. Non-reinforcing behaviors, or punishment, may not be a wise choice over the long term. Science has found that the use of these types of behaviors is most effective if one uses them each time an undesirable behavior occurs—difficult even under controlled laboratory circumstances. It has also been determined that non-reinforcing behaviors are most effective when they are used in combination with reinforcing behaviors.

Making the Point: Reinforcing Behavior

> Officer Davis and Officer Hayes have worked together for six years. They would describe their working relationship as really good. But these days, Officer Davis is frustrated with Officer Hayes' constant criticism about wanting to convert his religion to Buddhism. Officer Hayes also tends to make comments that lead Officer Davis to believe that he might not continue a friendship with him based on his religious views. Officer Davis and Officer Hayes have just eaten lunch and are sitting in the restaurant booth across from one another until it is time to go back in service.
>
> **Officer Hayes:** [Compassionate look on his face and sympathetic tone of voice] (*nonverbal reinforcer*) I really appreciate your patience about this whole Buddhism business. I just don't understand it and probably never will. Since I was raised Baptist, I'm just lost as to why you would want to do this. (*verbal reinforcer*)
>
> **Officer Davis:** [Smiles, looks down, shakes his head, and speaks with an amused tone] (*nonverbal reinforcer*) I'm glad you appreciate my patience, but it's wearing thin. (*verbal reinforcer and verbal non-reinforcer*)
>
> **Officer Hayes:** [Sympathetic smile and says in an assertive tone] (*nonverbal reinforcer*) I'll watch the comments that I make regarding your religion. I didn't mean to cause offense, buddy. I appreciate your patience and would never do anything to intentionally upset you. (*verbal reinforcer*)
>
> **Officer Davis:** [Looking uncertain and with a weary tone] (*nonverbal non-reinforcer*) I know it isn't easy for you, either. I know it is difficult to understand why I've decided to convert to Buddhism. I respect your views and opinions. (*verbal reinforcer*) But I'm losing patience about this. Your criticism about my new religion has got to stop, as my personal religious beliefs do not affect your or our friendship. You're the one who always brings it up and I've never tried

to force my beliefs on you. (*verbal non-reinforcer*) I hope you know that I still value our friendship, respect you and your opinions, and hope that we can still be friends (*verbal reinforcer*)

Summary of the Applications

Officers should continuously strive to develop professional skills to do a professional's job. Officers should lay to rest that familiar stereotype some citizens have of law enforcement as being over-authoritarian, uncaring and having a "just the facts" mentality.

The cornerstone of the social tactics skills that any law enforcement officer learns is decency—simple human decency! Officers have a job to do. But in doing it, they have to learn how to handle people like the human beings they are, and with the highest levels of dignity and respect. This process involves what has been called "the principle of reciprocal behavior"—a fancy way of saying that all people get back what they give. In the case of law enforcement officers, they have learned how to invest their work with professional effectiveness—with real skills—and still give people decent treatment.

About the Author

Stephen J. Sampson, Ph.D.

Dr. Steve Sampson has been teaching social intelligence and leadership skills for over 45 years. He has provided expert witness consulting to several law enforcement agencies on a national basis for 20 years.

As an **Educator**, he holds a Bachelor's Degree in Sociology from the University of Massachusetts (1970) and a Masters (1976) and Doctoral Degree (1981) in Counseling Psychology from Georgia State University. He is a nationally-recognized Master Trainer in Interpersonal Communication Skills since 1977, and has presented that training to over 300 agencies and organizations in 40 states. Dr. Sampson is a former Assistant Professor of Criminal Justice at Georgia State University from 1979 to 1985. In 2004, he retired from his position as a Clinical Professor in the Counseling Psychology at Georgia State University (1995–2004). He recently retired as Executive-in-Residence Professor at the College of Justice and Safety at Eastern Kentucky University (2009–present).

As a **Licensed Psychologist**, Dr. Sampson is the former Chief of Psychology of Georgia Regional Hospital, Atlanta, Georgia (1993–1995). He is also a nationally-recognized counseling psychologist who works with various law enforcement and public safety agencies conducting pre-screening potential candidates, psychological fitness for duty evaluations, and post shooting debriefings (since 1982). He currently owns a Psychological Services Company that provides contract services to over 50 Law Enforcement and Public Safety agencies in the state of Georgia. Dr. Sampson also has conducted management training (2003–2013) for several federal government agencies (FBI, NSA, DEA, USSS, DOE, FBOP, FLETC, and OPM).

As a **Criminologist**, Dr. Sampson is the former correctional superintendent for Massachusetts Halfway Houses Inc. (1969–1973), as well as a former Correctional Superintendent for the Georgia Department of Corrections (1973–1976). He has provided consulting services to over 100 law enforcement and correction agencies since 1980.

As an **Author**, Dr. Sampson has published the following books:

Social Intelligence Skills for Government Managers (HRD Press, Inc.)

Social Intelligence Skills for Law Enforcement Supervisors/ Managers (HRD Press, Inc.)

Social Intelligence Skills for Correctional Supervisors/ Managers (HRD Press, Inc.)

How to be in a Personal Relationship (HRD Press, Inc.)

Applied Social Intelligence (HRD Press, Inc.)

Leaders without Titles (HRD Press, Inc.)

Testimonials

"I have known Dr. Steve Sampson for over 20 years. During 18 of those years, he served as the LaGrange Police Department's psychologist for pre-employment consultation and critical incidents de-briefings. He has consistently provided a valuable service to our agency and to our officers. Additionally, Dr. Sampson provides leadership and interpersonal communications training for our leadership team and is a significant resource who is clearly committed to professional police services. Dr. Sampson has my complete confidence and I give him my highest recommendation."

Chief of Police Lou Dekmar (LaGrange PD)

"Steve Sampson focuses on the prerequisite qualities that can be developed and honed by individuals into effective leadership with a moral compass. In *Leaders without Titles*, Dr. Sampson provides a blueprint for the development of what he believes to be the six essential dimensions of leadership. Similar to all of his work, the material is presented in a practical, straightforward approach that not only allows the reader to understand the theoretical underpinnings of each dimension, but also practice the concepts involved. In order to gauge proficiency as the skills are being developed, a method for testing is provided. It is excellent."

**Dr. Allen Ault, Dean, College of Justice & Safety,
Eastern Kentucky University**

"I have known Dr. Steve Sampson for 25 years. He has been a successful professor in the Criminal Justice Department as well as the College of Education at Georgia State University. Dr. Sampson has assisted this department in Fitness for Duty evaluations of police officers. The Law Enforcement community throughout Georgia and the entire United States holds Dr. Sampson in high regard. I can unequivocally vouch for his character and his integrity."

**Chief of Police/Assistant Vice President Connie B. Sampson
(Georgia State University)**

"In any organizational environment, there are individuals to whom others look for guidance, direction, and leadership. Very often those persons are not the highest ranking members of the organization. Why? Dr. Sampson provides an insightful analysis of the complex array of factors that cause some people to become leaders while others can only manage. *Leaders without Titles* is a must-read to understand these critical dynamics."

Gary Deland, Executive Director (Utah Sheriff's Association)

"Dr. Sampson is an expert on developing social intelligence skills for leadership, and can adapt to any audience using practical applications to bring out the leaders within."

Dr. Winifred McPherson, Retired Major (Broward County Sheriff's Department)

"For over 25 years, Dr. Sampson has served and supported the Gwinnett County Police Department. Through training and counseling, he has provided our employees and their families with a tremendous resource. Dr. Sampson's efforts have enabled our employees to enjoy healthy, successful careers and enriched their personal lives."

Chief of Police Charles Walters (Gwinnett County Police Department, retired)

Made in the USA
Monee, IL
21 January 2020